For Maura and h...
Br...

MIDD...
VEGETARIAN COOKERY

A complement for
ambitious days and
those when you aren't
in the mood to chop
cheese.

Sarah

Rider books also by David Scott

Indonesian Cookery (with Surya Winata)
Protein-Rich Vegetarian Cookery
The Vegan Diet (with Claire Golding)
The Penniless Vegetarian
A Taste of Thailand (with Kristiaan Inwood)

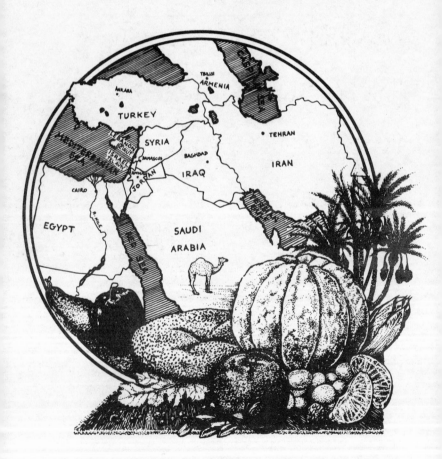

MIDDLE EASTERN
VEGETARIAN COOKERY

DAVID SCOTT

Illustrated by Steve Hardstaff

RIDER
LONDON • SYDNEY • AUCKLAND • JOHANNESBURG

First published in 1981 by Rider
An imprint of Random House Ltd
20 Vauxhall Bridge Road, London SW1V 2SA

Random House Australia (Pty) Ltd
20 Alfred Street, Milsons Point,
Sydney, NSW 2061, Australia

Random House New Zealand Ltd
18 Poland Road, Glenfield
Auckland 10, New Zealand

Random House Group South Africa (Pty) Ltd
PO Box 337, Bergvlei, South Africa

Reprinted 1982, 1983, 1986
This edition 1992
Reprinted 1993

Printed and bound in Great Britain by
The Guernsey Press Co. Ltd, Guernsey, Channel Islands

A catalogue record for this book is available
from the British Library.

ISBN 0-7126-5262-0

This book is printed on recycled paper.

CONTENTS

ACKNOWLEDGEMENTS

I would like to thank Maire Morgan for helping me test some of the recipes and for her assistance in correcting the text. Thanks also to Tim and Roberta for their company while I was writing the book and to New York City Library for the use of their excellent reference books on Middle Eastern cooking and customs.

INTRODUCTION

This book is concerned with the cooking of those countries which together are broadly described as the Middle East. They include Armenia, Egypt, Iran, Israel, Lebanon, Morocco, Syria and Turkey; countries with both histories and culinary arts that are inextricably linked. For thousands of years the Middle East has seen the rise and fall of a host of different cultures and religions. In an area rich in grains, pulses, fruits, vegetables, spices and herbs this has produced a fascinating mixture of cuisines with endless possibilities and variations. The wide range of ingredients traditionally used (e.g. rice, wheat, chick peas, lentils, many vegetables, dates, nuts, olives, dried and fresh fruits, yoghurt, cheeses and spices) has resulted in the creation of many delicious vegetarian dishes that are attractive to any person interested in imaginative, unusual and economical cooking. The recipes are not meatless in the conscious sense, but because they have developed naturally from the ingredients available. They dispose once and for all of the myth that one cannot be a lover of good food and at the same time enjoy a meal without meat.

The recipes in the book have been collected by me over a number of years in my work as a restaurateur and during trips to the Middle East. I have also studied many Middle Eastern cookery books, some of which are listed in the Bibliography. Most of the recipes are traditional, but a few include ingredients such as potatoes and avocado pears that have only recently but successfully been introduced to the area. The dishes are sometimes elaborate but most often simple and usually easy to prepare from ingredients readily available in both Britain and America. In Britain the occasional unusual ingredient can normally be found in a Greek or Indian grocery shop or delicatessen.

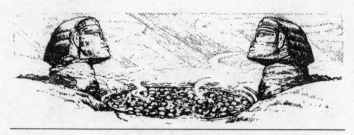

HISTORY

The Persian Empire of some five centuries BC was the earliest political entity to embrace all the countries in the geographical region known today as the Middle East. The region was later included in the Greek, Roman and Byzantine Empires. More changes took place after the death of the prophet Mohammed in the seventh century when the whole region, as well as areas further afield, was conquered by Moslem Arabs and converted to Islam.

Further integration was achieved by the Turkish Ottoman Empire which ruled from the early sixteenth century right up to the First World War, and by the beginning of the twentieth century Middle Eastern cooking had developed a common, recognizable style not unique to any one country.

These are the origins of Middle Eastern cooking, and most of the recipes given in the book can be found in various forms throughout the Middle East.

Persia, the old name for Iran, has been used when referring to the early history of that country.

NOTES TO THE COOK

In orthodox Middle Eastern cooking most recipes would normally have been carefully handed down from cook to cook and it would be a matter of pride that they were followed exactly as they had been taught. However, circumstances for the users of this book are very different and I would recommend you to follow the inclinations of your own taste buds and appetite and where necessary adjust recipes accordingly.

In general Middle Eastern food is quite mildly spiced and makes use of the aromatic and gently perfumed seasonings such as cinammon, cumin, cardamom and cloves. Hot, spicy food is not as common as in Indian cooking, perhaps its nearest neighbour in style. Fresh herbs, especially parsley and mint, are used frequently although the dried variety can be substituted if fresh ones are unavailable.

The following herbs, spices and other ingredients are required in many of the recipes, and it may be useful to have them available before starting to use the book.

Herbs

parsley, fresh if possible
mint, fresh if possible, although dried will often be satisfactory

Spices

black pepper	allspice
cinammon	turmeric
cumin	anise seeds
coriander	caraway seeds
cardamom	sesame seeds

Nuts

almonds
walnuts

Other ingredients

yoghurt
tahini
lemons
olive oil or other good vegetable oil
honey
chick peas
filo pastry (for some of the pastries)

N.B. All recipes are for 4 to 5 people unless stated otherwise.

SPECIAL NOTES
FOR AMERICAN COOKS

All measurements are given in imperial and metric. An easy-to-use American conversion table is given at the back of the book, which gives cup equivalents for those ingredients normally measured out that way by American cooks.

The following list will clarify any confusion that may arise because of the different cooking terms and ingredient names used in Britain and America.

English	*American*
aubergine	egg plant
biscuit	cookie
broil	grill
bulgar wheat	cracked wheat
courgettes	zucchini
frying pan	skillet
icing sugar	confectioners' sugar
marrow	squash
mince	ground
semolina	cream of wheat (or farina)
spring onions	scallions
tin	can
wholewheat flour	graham flour

GLOSSARY OF INGREDIENTS
AND COOKING TERMS

Alternative names are given in brackets after the most common name.

Almonds	Sweet almonds are used extensively in Middle Eastern cooking. They are cooked whole or used ground in puddings, cake and pastries
Ataif	pancakes similar to the French *crêpe*
Aubergine	(egg plant) plump, purple-skinned vegetable, member of the marrow family, used very often in Middle Eastern cooking
Baklava	(*pakhlava*) Turkish name for the paper-thin sheets of pastry known as *fila* in Greek cookery. Also the name of a sweet consisting of layers of the pastry buttered and filled with crushed nuts
Borek	(*boerag, burekas, boerek*) describes a large array of savoury or sweet pastries consisting of various fillings wrapped in a variety of pastries, e.g. *fila* pastry or flaky pastry or shortcrust; cheese, spinach and meat fillings are the most popular
Bulgar	(*burghal, bulghur,* cracked wheat) a wheat product made since ancient times in the Middle East and other parts of Western Asia: whole wheat grains are parboiled and then dried in the sun
Cayenne	a hot red pepper made from dried ground chilli peppers
Chelo	Iranian name for plain cooked rice
Chick peas	(*garbanzos*) corn-coloured, nut-like legumes uses in many traditional Middle Eastern dishes, notably *hummus bi tahini,* couscous and *falafel*; they need long soaking and cooking before use

Cinnamon	sweet, musky spice made from the dried inner bark of the cinnamon tree; used in savoury and sweet dishes
Coriander	mild, sweet spice; the crushed seed is used in casseroles, apple pies and particularly lentil dishes
Couscous	the national dish of Morocco, Tunisia and Algeria. It is the name of a grain product made from semolina and the name of a dish which includes couscous as an ingredient. Cooked couscous looks like large white grains of buckshot. It is served in a mountainous heap with a vegetable or meat or sweet sauce poured over the top.
Cracked wheat	see bulgar
Cumin	strong, aromatic spice used in seed form or crushed. Popular in curries; also used to flavour cheese dishes and pulses
Dolma	stuffed vegetables, usually meaning a rice mixture wrapped in vine or cabbage leaves
Falafel	chick pea croquettes. A favourite snack food in the Middle East, usually sold stuffed into pitta bread with a variety of sauces
Fila	(*filo, phyllo, yufka*) a paper-thin dough very popular throughout the Middle East and used in a variety of ways. It is very difficult to make and is usually bought pre-prepared. A 1 lb (454 g) package will normally contain 24 sheets of pastry measuring 20 x 24 in (50 x 60 cm)
Ful medames	large, brown beans, members of the kidney bean family. Very popular in Egypt, where they are served with hard-boiled eggs, lemon and parsley
Harissa	a hot sauce used to flavour and garnish couscous. It is made from cayenne pepper, ground cumin, garlic, salt and olive oil.
Helva	(*halva, halvak*) A type of flaky confection made from semolina, honey, butter, sesame seeds and almonds
Hummus bi tahini	a bread dip appetizer made from ground chick peas, garlic and tahini paste
Kadayif	(*kadaif, kanata*) A very common sweet pastry made from a shredded, vermicelli-like pastry. Filled with a nut mixture it is baked and then soaked in a sugar or honey syrup.

Khoresh	Iranian vegetable or meat sauces served with rice
Mast	Iranian for yoghurt
Matzo meal	a meal produced by crushing *matzo*, the Jewish unleavened bread. Very good for thickening soups and for making stuffings
Mezze	Middle Eastern hors d'oeuvres
Mint	a popular herb in Middle Eastern cooking. Used fresh in salads and dressings. Infused with green tea to give refreshing mint tea
Mishshi	stuffed vegetables
Olive oil	the traditional cooking oil and salad dressing of the Middle East. It had a distinctive taste. It is always used in dishes that will be served cold.
Paprika	red pepper made from dried, ground red capsicum peppers after the seeds and stalk have been removed. It is much milder than cayenne pepper
Parsley	much used in Middle Eastern cooking both as a garnish and a cooking herb. The stronger, longer-leaved French type is favoured
Pilav	(*pilaf, pilaff*) rice cooked with stock, spices, meat and/or vegetables. Sometimes the rice is parboiled before it is mixed with the other ingredients
Pine nuts	(*pignolias*) small white or cream-coloured nuts, soft in texture unless roasted, which grow inside the hard shell of pine cones. They are delicious and impart a distinctive flavour to any dish to which they are added
Pistachio	much prized green nut. Gives a unique flavour to any dish in which it is cooked. Used in both savoury and sweet recipes
Pitta bread	(*pita, pide*) staple bread of the Middle East. Prepared in a variety of ways but it is normally round and flat with a hollow or pouch in the middle. It is soft in texture and it is delicious with dips such as hummus or for mopping up sauces. Often the pitta is split in half and the pouch stuffed with salads or cooked food and eaten as a snack
Saffron	golden-coloured, slightly sweet stigma of crocuses. Sold in whole dried strands or powdered. Used for colouring and flavouring, particularly in rice dishes. It is expensive and turmeric is a cheaper alternative

Semolina   flour produced from the starchy centre of wheat grain. Various grades ranging from fine to coarse are available. Fine semolina is used to make puddings, while the coarse grades give a crumbly texture to cake mixtures. Couscous is made from coarse semolina

Sesame seeds   mild nut-flavoured seeds used to flavour savoury and sweet dishes. Toasted seeds are sprinkled on breads and biscuits, and are also the main ingredient of a number of sweet pastries. Tahini paste is made from the crushed seeds

Tahini   (*tahina*) a paste made from sesame seeds. Used to make salad dressings and dips

Turmeric   a bright yellow powder slightly sour in taste, used to colour rice dishes

Vine leaves   used fresh in countries where grapes grow, or tinned abroad. Stuffed with a rice mixture, they are a popular appetizer

Zucchini   another name for courgettes

MEZZE (HORS D'OEUVRES)
INCLUDING YOGHURT MAKING

Mezze or Middle Eastern hors d'oeuvres make up some of my favourite dishes and I am always happier to eat a selection of *mezze* accompanied by warm pitta bread and a glass of beer than an elaborate meal. For the hostess or host, one or two mezze can make an excellent snack for the unexpected guest, while a larger number can provide the basis for an exciting buffet. Freshly sliced cucumber, tomatoes with feta cheese, cooked spinach in yoghurt, fried or baked aubergine, hummus, cold bean stew or stuffed vine leaves are some of the foods served. Salads, pickles and small savoury pastries which are also served as *mezze* are discussed in later chapters.

Consider contrasts in colour and texture when deciding which *mezze* to prepare, and present them garnished with fresh herbs, small bowls of olives, roasted nuts and wedges of lemon.

Simple mezze

Quartered tomatoes. Olives. Nuts. Fresh raw vegetables chopped and sprinkled with finely chopped herbs and onion. Almonds in their skins, sprinkled with salty water and baked in the oven until browned. Chick peas or other pulses soaked, drained and then just salted. Olives in a lemon and oil dressing. Olives, stoned and then crushed with 1 or 2 cloves of garlic. Thin slices of cucumber lightly sprinkled with fresh mint and/or lemon juice. Thin onion slices. A bowl of chopped parsley. Lemon wedges. Pickled vegetables. Avocados with salad dressing or yoghurt or sour cream. Cottage or curd cheese sprinkled with cumin seeds and served on lettuce leaves.

Roasted mixed nuts (ajeel)

Combine a selection of the following: almonds, hazelnuts, walnuts, pistachios, pine nuts, pumpkin seeds, watermelon seeds. Place in a pan and just cover with equal quantities of water and lemon juice and boil. Reduce heat, add salt to taste and simmer for 10 minutes. Drain, spread the mixture out on a flat baking sheet and roast the nuts gently in a hot oven, 450° F (230° C, gas mark 7) until just browned.

Bread dips

Various dips, purées and cream salads are served as appetizers with pitta bread. They can also be used as dressings for hot or cold vegetables or salads, or as accompaniments to main dishes.

Tahini dips

Tahini is a sesame paste made by blending a mixture of equal volumes of sesame seed and water. It is a common ingredient in dips and dressings. Tahini itself is invariably bought ready prepared. Below are two recipes for dips made with tahini – the second is sharper and contains more garlic than the first. A recipe for chick peas with tahini (*hummus bi tahini*) is given on p. 19.

Recipe 1

8 fl oz (225 ml) tahini
2 cloves garlic, crushed
4 fl oz (100 ml) water
juice of 2 lemons

3 tablespoons vegetable oil
   (olive oil is traditionally used)
salt to taste
2 tablespoons chopped parsley
pinch of cayenne

Blend or thoroughly mix the tahini, garlic, water, lemon juice and oil. Add more water if the dip is too thick, and then add salt to taste. Serve garnished with parsley and a sprinkling of cayenne.

Recipe 2

8 fl oz (225 ml) tahini
juice of 3 lemons
3 cloves garlic, crushed
2 tablespoons vegetable oil
   (olive oil is traditionally used)

3 tablespoons finely chopped
   fresh herbs (e.g. parsley,
   mint, coriander, dill)
water
salt to taste

Combine the first five ingredients and blend or whisk to a smooth paste. Add water to achieve the desired thickness and add salt to taste before serving. For tahini and yoghurt dip replace the water with 4 fl oz (100 ml) of yoghurt.

Chick pea and yoghurt dip

8 oz (225 g) chick peas, tinned
　or cooked soft
4 fl oz (100 ml) yoghurt
juice of 1 lemon

1 teaspoon crushed dried mint
salt and black pepper to taste
rind of ½ a lemon, grated

Blend together the first four ingredients. Season the mixture to taste with salt and black pepper, and thin down with water if it's too thick. Serve garnished with grated lemon peel. Diced green pepper and/or celery added to the dip after it has been made gives it a pleasant crunchy texture.

Chick peas in yoghurt and French dressing

Follow the previous recipe but add 4 tablespoons of vegetable oil and 2 tablespoons of vinegar to the ingredients.

Aubergine and tahini dip

2 small aubergines
4 fl oz (100 ml) tahini
juice of 1 lemon
1 clove garlic, crushed

2 tablespoons finely chopped
　fresh parsley
salt to taste

Place the aubergines under a moderately hot grill and sear them all over under the flame. The skins should turn black and bubbly while the flesh inside becomes soft and tender. Alternatively lightly oil the aubergines and place them in an oven preheated to 350° F (175° C gas mark 4) for about 1 hour or until the aubergine interiors are well cooked. Rub or peel the skins off (the job is most easily done holding the aubergine under a cold tap). Combine the aubergine flesh with the remaining ingredients and either beat together or blend into a smooth paste. Serve garnished with black olives.

Aubergine purée dip

2 small aubergines
2 cloves garlic, crushed
juice of 1 lemon
3 tablespoons vegetable oil

salt and black pepper to taste
2 tablespoons finely chopped
    fresh parsley

Cook and peel the aubergines as described in the recipe above. Blend the flesh with all the remaining ingredients except the parsley, and before serving adjust the taste to your liking by adding more garlic or lemon, etc. Serve garnished with parsley. For extra texture and flavour stir into the purée before serving 2 oz (50 g) toasted sesame seeds.

Aubergine and yoghurt purée dip

Proceed as for aubergine purée dip (above) but add 6 fl oz (175 ml) yoghurt to the ingredients.

Fried aubergine and onion spread

1 large aubergine, cut into ½
    in (1.3 cm) slices
3 tablespoons vegetable oil
    (olive oil is best)

flour or breadcrumbs
1 small onion, diced finely
salt and black pepper to taste
vinegar or lemon juice to taste

Salt the aubergine slices, place them in a colander and leave pressed under a weight for 30 minutes. Rinse, drain and pat dry. Dip the slices in flour or some fine breadcrumbs and fry in 2 tablespoons of oil in a heavy frying pan until nicely browned on both sides. Remove the slices and leave to drain on absorbent paper. Add the remaining oil to the pan and fry the onion golden brown. Combine the aubergine slices, onion, salt and black pepper and gently mash them together. Add vinegar or lemon juice to taste. Chill and serve.

Avocado purée dip

This is worth making when the greengrocer is selling blackened, over-ripe avocados very cheaply. The dip is very rich and you may wish to make only half the quantity given in the recipe.

2 ripe avocados

juice and grated rind of 1 lemon

2 cloves garlic, crushed

salt and black pepper to taste

up to 5 fl oz (150 ml) vegetable
    oil (olive oil is best)

Put the avocado flesh, lemon peel, lemon juice and garlic into a blender (or mix by hand) and make a smooth paste. Leaving the paste in the blender, add salt and black pepper to taste. Now put the blender on the slowest speed and slowly add the oil. Stop when the mixture stops absorbing oil or when the taste is to your liking.

Chick peas with tahini (hummus bi tahini)

Hummus is probably the most popular and best known of the Middle Eastern bread dips. There are many recipes but they are mostly very similar, differing only in the relative quantities of tahini, garlic and lemon juice. The hummus is served with small bowls of olive oil, paprika, chopped parsley and sometimes pine nuts browned in butter as garnishes and with side dishes of pitta bread, olives and a fresh salad.

If you do not have time to soak and cook dried chick peas, try using tinned ones. They make a very good substitute and are now quite common in the shops. If by mistake you make the hummus too thin it can be thickened by stirring in some cottage cheese or even ground nuts.

8 oz (225 g) chick peas, soaked
    overnight, drained

2 pt (1.1 l) water

juice of 2 lemons

5 fl oz (150 ml) tahini

3 cloves garlic, crushed

salt to taste

Garnishes

olive oil

paprika

chopped parsley

Put the chick peas in a heavy pot with the water and bring to the boil. Remove any foam that forms and gently boil the peas for 1 to 1½ hours or until they are very soft. Drain and reserve any cooking liquid. The hummus can now be prepared, either using an electric blender, or by hand with a mouli or a pestle and mortar.

Electric blender method

Put the cooked peas, oil, lemon juice, garlic and tahini into the blender with enough cooking liquid or plain water to allow the mixture to purée satisfactorily. Add salt to taste and more lemon juice or tahini as necessary after the first tasting. Blend again, and it's ready to be served.

Hand method

Press the cooked peas through a sieve or the fine blade of a mouli, or crush in a pestle and mortar. Crush the garlic with some salt and add to the chick pea paste. Stir in the tahini, lemon juice and enough cooking liquid or plain water to form a smooth, creamy paste. Add salt to taste and adjust the quantities of lemon juice and tahini as required.

Pour the prepared hummus on to a serving dish, sprinkle paprika and chopped parsley over the top and pour over 1 or 2 tablespoons of olive oil.

Chick pea and cumin seed dip

8 oz (225 g) chick peas, soaked overnight and drained
2 teaspoons cumin seeds
2 fl oz (50 ml) vegetable oil (olive oil is best)

juice of 2 lemons
2 cloves garlic, crushed
salt and pepper to taste
chopped fresh mint or parsley for garnish

Put the chick peas in a heavy pan, just cover with water, add the cumin seeds, cover and cook over a moderate heat until the chick peas are very soft (about 1 hour). Remove any froth that forms and keep the peas covered by liquid during cooking. Put the chick peas, cooking water and remaining ingredients (except the garnish) in an electric blender or press through a mouli to give a nice creamy dip. Adjust seasoning and thin with water if the dip is too thick, garnish with chopped mint or parsley and serve.

Fried cheese with olives

Hot, fried cubes of cheese served with a light sprinkling of lemon juice are delicious. In this Egyptian recipe the cheese is fried in butter with olives. Serve with fresh bread and slices of lemon.

1 tablespoon butter
8 oz (225 g) firm or hard cheese cut into ½ in (1.3 cm) cubes

10–15 black olives, halved and pitted

Melt the butter in a small, heavy frying pan and add the cheese and olives. Fry gently, turning the cheese cubes frequently until they are very hot all the way through. Serve immediately.

Falafel or ta'amia

Ta'amia and *falafel* are spicy, deep fried bean croquettes. In Egypt, *ta'amia* made from dried white broad beans are a national dish. The idea was imported to Israel where they substituted chick peas and called the croquettes *falafel*. In both countries they are popular snack foods sold stuffed into split pitta bread, dressed with a hot sauce and accompanied by pickled vegetables. This recipe is for *falafel*, since chick peas are easier to obtain than Egyptian white beans.

8 oz (225 g) chick peas, soaked
  overnight and drained
2 cloves garlic, crushed
2 medium onions, finely diced
1 bunch parsley, finely chopped
1 teaspoon ground coriander

1 teaspoon ground cumin
½ teaspoon turmeric
¼ teaspoon cayenne
½ teaspoon baking powder
salt and black pepper to taste
vegetable oil for deep frying

Cover the chick peas in water and cook until soft (about 1 hour). Drain, and reserve the water for a soup, if you wish. Now mash the chick peas to a paste, which can be done by hand using a mincer or pestle and mortar, or in an electric blender. Combine the paste with the remaining ingredients (except the deep frying oil) and mix them together thoroughly. Leave this mixture to rest for 30 minutes and then form into 14 to 16 balls. If the balls are sticky, roll them in a little flour. Deep fry them in hot oil until brown and crisp. Drain on absorbent paper, and serve hot with one of the dips given earlier in the chapter or with the hot sauce or relish given below, a green salad and pickles. Alternatively stuff the *falafel* into pieces of split pitta bread and pour over the sauce or relish or another dressing.

The baking powder can be replaced by the same weight of dried yeast. If yeast is used, prove it with a little sugar and warm water before adding it to the other ingredients, and leave the *falafel* mixture for 1 hour rather than 30 minutes before cooking.

Cooked mashed vegetables, chopped nuts, caraway seeds or other ingredients may be added to the *falafel* ingredients for more variety.

Falafel hot sauce

1 lb (450 g) tinned tomatoes
juice of 1 lemon
3 cloves garlic, crushed
1 tablespoon finely chopped
  parsley

1 teaspoon brown sugar
chilli sauce to taste
salt to taste

Put all the ingredients into a small, heavy pan, bring to the boil and simmer uncovered until the tomatoes break up (about 30 minutes). Adjust the seasoning and allow to cool.

Falafel relish

2 ripe tomatoes, peeled
¼ medium cucumber, finely diced
1 green pepper, seeded, cored and finely diced
2 tablespoons finely chopped parsley
salt, black pepper and chilli sauce to taste

Mash the tomatoes and combine with the other ingredients. Mix thoroughly and chill.

Lentil and bulgar croquettes

Serves 6 to 8.

Although *falafel* (see previous recipe) are delicious, they are quite troublesome to make and also, since they are deep fried, if they are being served as a starter they need the cook's attention at the beginning of the meal. In contrast these Armenian lentil cakes are easy to prepare and normally served cold. The unusual combination of lentils and bulgar wheat gives the croquettes a pleasant texture and flavour.

4 oz (100 g) butter or margarine
2 medium onions, finely diced
12 oz (350 g) split lentils
1¼ pt (675 ml) water
6 oz (175 g) fine bulgar wheat
2 tablespoons finely chopped parsley
salt and black pepper to taste
1 small bunch spring onions, chopped

Melt the butter in a heavy frying pan, add the onions and sauté golden brown. Set aside. Put the water and lentils in a heavy pot and bring to the boil. Reduce heat and cook for 15 minutes or until the lentils are soft. Add the bulgar wheat, onions and butter, parsley, black pepper and salt to taste. Stir the mixture over moderate heat for 2 to 3 minutes and then allow it to cool. Form the mixture into small patties (wet your hands if it sticks too much) and arrange them on a bed of lettuce. Garnish the patties with chopped spring onions and serve.

Potato fingers

Serve these Turkish hors d'oeuvres with a spicy tomato dipping sauce (see falafel hot sauce, p. 21) or just on their own with chilled crisp lettuce leaves and a salad dressing.

1 lb (450 g) potatoes, peeled	1 egg, beaten
6 oz (150 g) Cheddar cheese, grated	salt and black pepper to taste
1 oz (25 g) flour	oil for frying

Boil and drain the potatoes and mash them well. Add the cheese, flour and beaten egg and season generously. Knead the mixture well and form into finger-shaped rolls. Shallow fry in hot oil, drain on absorbent paper and serve.

Cucumber and yoghurt (cacik)

This appetizer is very refreshing on a hot day, or as an accompaniment to a spicy dish. The yoghurt dressing is identical to the drink called *aryan*, sold in the streets of Turkey during the summer.

12 fl oz (350 ml) yoghurt	salt to taste
2 teaspoons crushed dried mint, *or*	1 cucumber, peeled, sliced and diced
3 tablespoons finely chopped fresh mint	2 or 3 cloves garlic (optional)

Put the yoghurt in a bowl, add mint and salt, beat with a whisk until smooth and quite thin. Add a little water if necessary. Stir in the cucumber and chill. If garlic is added, crush it with a little salt.

Cucumber with feta cheese dressing

An Egyptian salad or appetizer often served with the bean salad *ful medames*. It is particularly delicious made with very fresh feta cheese, but cottage cheese is an acceptable substitute.

1 cucumber, thinly sliced	2 tablespoons olive oil
1 medium onion (as mild as possible), thinly sliced	juice of 1 lemon
a few lettuce leaves	½ teaspoon crushed dried oregano
4 oz (100 g) feta cheese	salt and pepper to taste

Arrange the cucumber and onion slices on the lettuce leaves. Blend or beat the remaining ingredients together and pour over. Serve immediately. An alternative method is to chop the cheese up by hand, then mix in the olive oil, lemon juice and oregano, and combine the mixture with the cucumber and onion slices. Sprinkle with salt and pepper and serve on a bed of lettuce leaves.

Baked stuffed aubergines (imam bayeldi)

This is a well-known Turkish dish. Its name means the imam who fainted. It's not known whether he fainted because the dish was so delicious, or because he thought his wife was being extravagant making such a rich dish for a humble man of God. Whatever, I hope you can enjoy it without any pangs of conscience. The dish can be served as a starter or as a main meal. In the former case the aubergines are cut into small portions before serving.

2 medium aubergines
4 fl oz (100 ml) olive oil
2 medium onions, finely
  chopped
1 medium green pepper, seeded
  and finely chopped

2 cloves garlic
2 tomatoes, chopped
1 bunch parsley, chopped
salt and black pepper to taste
juice 1 lemon
water

Wash the aubergines and cut the stems off. Cut them lengthwise into halves, and make a deep slit down the centre of each piece. Put the aubergines in a colander, salt them generously and set aside for 30 minutes. Now wash, drain and pat them dry. Using a little of the oil, lightly brown each half in a heavy frying pan and set aside. Add half the remaining oil to the frying pan and put in the onions, green pepper and garlic. Sauté and stir the mixture until the onions are nicely softened. Add the tomatoes and parsley and cook for a further 2 or 3 minutes.

Season to taste with salt and black pepper. Arrange the aubergine halves in a baking dish and tightly pack the slash in each one with the onion and tomato filling. Sprinkle over the remaining oil and pour into the dish the lemon juice and enough water to come two-thirds the way up the side of the stuffed aubergines. Cover the dish and simmer gently near the top of the oven for 1 hour or until the aubergines are soft and well cooked. Allow to cool and serve cold. Alternatively, cover the stuffed aubergines with a tomato sauce and bake covered in a preheated oven, 375° F (190° C, gas mark 5) for 1 hour. Other fillings besides the one given may be used – see stuffed vegetables, pp. 104–13.

Persian aubergine hors d'oeuvre

2 medium aubergines	8 fl oz (225 ml) yoghurt
2 fl oz (50 ml) vegetable oil	salt and pepper to taste

Peel the aubergines and cut them into ½ in thick slices. Put the slices in a colander and generously salt them. Set aside for 30 minutes. Now wash and drain them and pat them dry. Fry the slices in the oil in a heavy frying pan until well cooked and brown on both sides. Season the yoghurt and pour half into a bowl. Arrange the aubergine slices on top and pour over them the remaining yoghurt. Chill and serve. If you wish, garnish with a little parsley or mint.

Fried aubergine slices

2 small aubergines, cut into ⅜ in (1 cm) thick slices	2 cloves garlic, thinly sliced
4 fl oz (100 ml) olive oil	2 tablespoons vinegar
	salt to taste

Put the aubergine slices in a colander and generously salt them. Set aside for 30 minutes. Now wash and drain them and pat them dry. Fry the slices in the oil in a heavy frying pan until they are soft and browned on both sides. Layer the slices in a shallow dish, sprinkling each layer with garlic slices, vinegar and salt to taste. Chill and serve.

Fried courgettes

4 small courgettes, sliced lengthwise	2 cloves garlic
2 tablespoons vegetable oil (olive oil if possible)	salt to taste
	2 tablespoons vinegar

To make this Turkish dish, put the courgette slices in a colander and salt them generously. Set aside for 30 minutes. Now wash and rinse them and pat them dry. Heat the oil in a heavy frying pan, add the garlic and sauté lightly. Put in the courgette slices and brown them on both sides. Place them in a serving dish, season with salt and sprinkle the vinegar over them. Serve hot.

Roasted green peppers

4 medium green peppers	2 tablespoons olive oil
1 large clove garlic, thinly sliced	1 tablespoon vinegar
	salt to taste

This is a recipe from Armenia. Wash the peppers and carefully dry them. Grill (broil) each whole pepper separately under a moderate flame, turning 2 or 3 times until the skins are lightly charred. Rub or peel the skins off and cut off the stem end of each pepper. Remove the core and the seeds. Quarter each pepper lengthwise and arrange the quarters in a serving dish. Sprinkle over them the garlic, olive oil, vinegar and salt and set aside to chill.

Cold bean stew (fassoulia plaki)

The English translation of this dish's name doesn't make it sound particularly attractive, but it is in fact delicious and also economical to make. If you make more than you need it will keep for several days in a refrigerator and actually improves with age.

8 oz (225 g) haricot beans, soaked overnight and drained	2 tablespoons finely chopped parsley
1½ pt (850 ml) water	2 medium tomatoes, chopped
1 medium carrot, diced	1 tablespoon tomato paste
1 stick celery, chopped	salt and pepper to taste
1 medium potato, diced	3 fl oz (75 ml) vegetable oil
1 medium onion, sliced	(olive oil if possible)
2 cloves garlic, crushed	

Put the beans in a heavy pot, add the water and bring to the boil. Remove any froth, reduce the heat, cover and simmer for 1 hour. Add the remaining ingredients except the olive oil and simmer for 30 to 40 minutes. Add the oil and cook a further 15 minutes or longer. Leave to cool, and serve cold.

Stuffed vine leaves (dolmades)

Dolmades is a general name for stuffed vegetables, although the name normally refers to stuffed vine leaves. Each country has its own favourite dolmades filling and there is really no definitive recipe. A recipe for one filling is given below and more may be found in the section on stuffed vegetables, p. 104.

8 oz (225 g) tinned or packet
vine leaves or a bunch of
fresh leaves

juice of 2 lemons

Filling
1 medium onion, finely diced
2 tablespoons vegetable oil
8 oz (225 g) uncooked rice,
washed and drained
2 oz (50 g) currants
2 oz (50 g) pine nuts or
chopped walnuts

1 teaspoon allspice
1 teaspoon ground cinnamon
salt and black pepper to taste
1 tablespoon tomato paste

Fry the onion in the oil in a heavy pan until it is soft and transparent. Add the rice and fry, stirring all the time, for 2 to 3 minutes. Add enough water to cover the rice and then stir in all the remaining ingredients, except the tomato paste. Gently cook until the rice is cooked (add a little more water if needed) and all the moisture is absorbed. Stir in the tomato paste and remove from the heat.

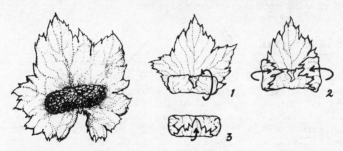

Meanwhile put the tinned or packet leaves in a bowl and scald with boiling water. Leave them to soak and disentangle themselves. Put the leaves in a colander and rinse with cold water. If you are using fresh leaves merely wash them and carefully cut out the central vein. Place a teaspoon or more of filling into the centre of each vine leaf. Roll the leaf over the filling, tucking in the sides as you go. Put some damaged leaves in the base of a heavy pot and layer the stuffed leaves on top. If you have more than one layer, separate each of the layers with vine leaves. Place an inverted saucer over the dolmades. Then add enough water just to cover them, add the lemon juice and cover the pot. Simmer for about 1 hour over a low heat. Alternatively, bake the dolmades in a low oven (300° F, 148° C, gas mark 2) for approximately 2 hours. Allow them to cool in the pot. Drain and arrange them on a serving tray. Chill and serve.

Yoghurt

Yoghurt is an excellent food. It's nourishing, good for the digestion, and versatile, and in the Middle East, where the climate for much of the year is hot, it solves the problem of storing fresh milk. Yoghurt also has the reputation of promoting longevity and for being a good stamina food. It is used in the preparation of *mezze*, soups and salads as a marinating agent, in main meals and in desserts, and even as a summer drink mixed with water, a pinch of salt and mint.

Home-made yoghurt is easy, and is much fresher, tastier and more economical than the shop-bought variety. The process simply involves the addition of live yoghurt to a batch of sterilized plain milk maintained at blood temperature (98° F, 37° C). The first source of live yoghurt can be bought at any health or wholefood store, and after that you just reserve some of your home-made yoghurt for use in making your next batch.

Making yoghurt at home possesses some of the mystique attached to breadmaking, but it is basically a simple and foolproof process. Here is a method that should always work.

Making yoghurt

Put 1 to 2 pints (500 ml to 1 l) of fresh milk (depending on how much you want to make) in a clean saucepan and bring to the boil. As soon as it bubbles, switch off the heat and transfer the milk to a clean ceramic or glass bowl. Allow the milk to cool to about blood temperature (98 to 100° F, 37 to 38° C). To test, put your finger into the milk, which should feel comfortably warm. If you like you can use a thermometer, although I never do. Now stir in 1 to 2 tablespoons of live yoghurt, cover the bowl with a lid and wrap the whole thing in a thick towel. Store in a warm place (e.g. the airing cupboard, above the pilot light on a gas stove, above the hot area at the back of the fridge, in the sun or near a radiator; some people pour the cultured milk into a thermos flask). Leave to set for 10 to 12 hours, when the yoghurt will be ready for use. Store in a refrigerator.

For a thick yoghurt, add 1 to 2 tablespoons of powdered milk to the fresh milk before starting. If you want to make a really large amount of yoghurt make it in several smaller batches rather than in one huge quantity. For some reason it seems to work better that way.

Finally, your first attempt at yoghurt making may produce quite a thin, runny yoghurt. Don't worry – this is quite usual, and it will get thicker the third or fourth time of making as your own culture improves.

Yoghurt cheese

This is an excellent cheese to use in sauces and stuffing mixtures for vegetables as well as in salads. It can be made from yoghurt that has gone a little too sharp for normal use. For a mild cheese, fresh yoghurt should be used.

2 pt (1 l) yoghurt
½ teaspoon salt
muslin bag

Put the yoghurt and salt into a bowl and stir well. Pour the mixture into a muslin or cheesecloth bag and leave to strain, hanging over a bowl, overnight. Discard the liquid. The cheese in the bag should be soft and creamy. For a firmer cheese leave it hanging longer.

SOUPS

Middle Eastern soups can be simple or exotic, and the ingredients used will depend on availability and occasion. The soups are often substantial, and vegetables, grains, pulses, yoghurt and even dried fruits will sometimes all be put in together. Soup is not usually served at the beginning of a meal as in the West, but is served as a main dish, particularly in cold weather.

Moroccan soup (harira)

During the month-long fast of Ramadan Moslems must observe a fast between sunrise and sunset, or, as instructed in the Koran: 'Eat and drink until so much dawn appears that a white thread may be distinguished from a black thread, then fast completely until night.' In Morocco a thick, nourishing soup called *harira* is traditionally served to break the fast. There are many recipes and each family has its favourite method. Below are two variations. *Harira* may be served as a first course or with bread and dates or dried figs as a main dish.

Chick pea harira

Serves 6 to 8

8 oz (225 g) chick peas, soaked
 overnight and drained
1 medium onion, diced
2 oz (50 g) butter or vegetable
 oil
1 small bunch parsley, finely
 chopped
½ teaspoon turmeric or saffron
1 teaspoon ground cinnamon

5 pt (3 l) water
salt and black pepper to taste
4 oz (100 g) rice, washed and
 drained
3 tablespoons flour
6 fl oz (175 ml) water
2 eggs, lightly beaten (optional)
juice of 1 lemon

Put the first six ingredients into a heavy pot and stir over a medium heat for 3 to 4 minutes. Add the 5pt (3 l) water and bring to the boil. Cover, reduce heat and simmer until the chick peas are cooked (about 1 hour). Season to taste with salt and black pepper and add the rice. Return to the boil, reduce the heat and simmer until the rice is cooked. Now, beat the flour and 6 fl oz (175 ml) water into a smooth paste and stir into the soup. Continue cooking, stirring occasionally, for a further 15 minutes and then remove the soup from the heat. Adjust the seasoning, add water if needed and, if you wish, stir in the lightly beaten eggs. Add the lemon juice and leave the soup to stand for a few minutes or until the egg is cooked.

Mixed bean harira

Serves 6 to 8

4 oz (100 g) haricot beans,
  soaked overnight and drained
4 oz (100 g) chick peas, soaked
  overnight and drained
4 oz (100 g) whole brown or
  green lentils, washed and
  drained
5 pt (3 l) water
1 lb (450 g) fresh tomatoes,
  quartered, or tinned tomatoes

1 medium onion, diced
½ teaspoon turmeric or saffron
1 teaspoon ground coriander
salt and black pepper to taste
3 tablespoons flour
6 fl oz (175 ml) water
juice of 1 lemon

Put the haricot beans, chick peas, lentils and 5 pt (3 l) water in a heavy pot, bring to the boil, reduce the heat, cover and simmer until the pulses are tender (about 1 hour). Add the tomatoes, onions, turmeric and coriander, and season to taste with salt and black pepper. Return to simmer and leave to cook for 30 minutes. Beat the flour and 6 fl oz (175 ml) water into a smooth paste and stir into the soup. Add more water as necessary and cook a further 15 minutes or until the pulses are really soft and just starting to break up. Adjust the seasoning, stir in the lemon juice and serve.

Egg and lemon soup

Egg yolks are the thickening agent in this popular Middle Eastern soup. Once they have been added the soup should not be allowed to boil or the yolks will curdle. For a thinner soup halve the quantity of rice.

2 tablespoons vegetable oil
1 medium onion, diced
4 oz (100 g) rice, washed and
  drained
2¼ pt (1.3 l) water or stock
salt and black pepper to taste

juice of 1 medium or 2 small
  lemons
2 egg yolks
1 tablespoon chopped fresh
  parsley

Heat the oil in a heavy pan and sauté the onion until lightly browned. Stir in the rice and sauté over a moderate heat for 1 or 2 minutes. Add the water or stock and season to taste with salt and black pepper. Bring to the boil, reduce the heat and simmer until the rice is cooked. Remove from the heat. Beat the egg yolks and lemon juice together in a bowl and slowly stir in some of the soup. Blend the mixture thoroughly and return it to the rest of soup. Carefully reheat the soup until it thickens, not allowing it to come to the boil. Adjust the seasoning, and serve the soup garnished with parsley. On a hot day the soup can be served chilled and garnished with chopped fresh mint rather than parsley. Sometimes spinach is added to this soup. If you wish to try it, add 8 oz (225 g) chopped spinach at the same time as the water.

Red bean and spinach soup

Serves 6 to 8

This is a rich and nourishing Iranian soup which may be served as a main meal.

8 oz (225 g) red beans, soaked
  overnight and drained
1 pt (575 ml) water
4 tablespoons vegetable oil
2 medium onions, diced
½ teaspoon turmeric
pinch of cayenne
8 oz (225 g) lentils, washed and
  drained

4 oz (100 g) rice, washed and
  drained
3 pt (1.75 l) water
salt and black pepper to taste
1 lb (450 g) fresh spinach,
  washed and chopped
juice of 2 lemons
yoghurt for garnishing
  (optional)

Put the beans and 1 pt (575 ml) water in a heavy pot and cook until they are just tender. You may need to add more water during cooking. Transfer the beans and cooking liquid to another container, clean the pot out and add the vegetable oil. Add the onions and sauté over moderate heat until just brown. Stir in the turmeric, cayenne, lentils and rice and sauté, stirring, for a further minute or two. Pour in the 3 pt (1.75 ml) water and reserved beans, plus cooking liquid. Season to taste with salt and black pepper and bring to the boil. Reduce heat, cover and simmer for 45 minutes. Now add the spinach and more turmeric and cayenne if needed. Return to the boil, reduce heat, cover and simmer a further 15 minutes. Stir in the lemon juice, leave for 2 to 3 minutes on the heat, and then serve. The soup may be garnished with yoghurt if desired.

Spicy hot mixed bean soup

Serves 6 to 8

2 oz (50 g) chick peas	1 tablespoon tomato paste
2 oz (50 g) lentils	1 chilli pepper, chopped
2 oz (50 g) *ful medames* or other	4 oz (100 g) mashed potato
brown beans	salt to taste
2 oz (50 g) barley	yoghurt to taste
3 pt (175 l) water or stock	

Combine the chick peas, lentils and *ful medames*, cover with water and leave to soak overnight. Drain. Put the mixed beans and lentils in a heavy pan, add the water or stock, tomato paste and chili pepper and bring to the boil. Reduce heat, cover and simmer until the beans and barley are soft. Stir in the mashed potato, season to taste with salt and simmer a further 10 minutes. Serve with a bowl of yoghurt which should be spooned into the soup as desired.

Borsch soup

This soup, more normally associated with Eastern European countries, is also well known in Turkey. There are differences in the way the soup is prepared in the two regions – notably in the Turkish version the vegetables are not puréed before the soup is served.

1 oz (25 g) butter or margarine	2 cloves garlic, crushed
1 lb (450 g) raw beetroots,	3 pt (1.75 l) boiling water
peeled and diced small	8 oz (225 g) tinned tomatoes
2 medium onions, diced	½ teaspoon crushed dill seeds
2 sticks celery, sliced	salt and black pepper to taste
2 medium potatoes, peeled and	juice of 1 lemon
diced	8 fl oz (225 g) sour cream or
1 medium green pepper,	yoghurt
seeded, cored and sliced	

Melt the butter in a heavy saucepan and add all the vegetables and the crushed garlic. Sauté, stirring, for a few minutes and then add the boiling water, tomatoes and dill seeds. Season with salt and black pepper, bring to the boil, reduce heat, cover and simmer for 2 hours or until all the vegetables are very tender. Pour the soup into a tureen, stir in the lemon juice and serve with a bowl of sour cream or yoghurt or a mixture of the two.

Onion soup

Onion soup is popular in Iran and Turkey. Its preparation is similar to French onion soup, but the seasoning is different. The soup may be served with croûtons and grated cheese; alternatively lightly beaten eggs can be whipped into it just before serving.

2 oz (50 g) butter or vegetable oil
1 lb (450 g) onions, thinly sliced
1 oz (25 g) flour
3–4 pt (2 l) water
salt and black pepper to taste
½ teaspoon turmeric

1 teaspoon sugar
juice of 1 lemon
2 teaspoons dried mint
½ teaspoon ground cinnamon
2 eggs, lightly beaten, *or* slices of French bread and 4 oz (100 g) Parmesan cheese

Melt the butter or oil in a heavy pan and add the onions. Cook with occasional stirring for 15 minutes over gentle heat. Use a little of the water to make a paste with the flour and stir this into the onions. Stirring constantly, continue to cook the onion and flour mixture for 2 to 3 minutes. Add the water and bring to the boil. Reduce heat and season to taste with salt and black pepper. Add the turmeric, sugar and lemon juice, cover and leave to simmer for 45 minutes or longer. Adjust the seasoning. Rub the mint to a powder and mix with the cinnamon. Stir the mixture into the soup and remove from the heat. Now stir in the 2 lightly beaten eggs and serve. Alternatively, leave out the eggs and lightly toast the slices of French bread, put one piece in each bowl, pour the soup over them, and serve with Parmesan cheese.

Lentil soup

This popular soup has many variations. Two methods are given below. These are different in both texture and taste and you should try both. Red, brown or green lentils can be used. If you wish to speed up the cooking time soak the lentils before use.

Recipe 1

2 fl oz (50 g) butter or
  vegetable oil
1 large onion, chopped
2 cloves garlic, crushed
1 medium carrot, peeled and
  sliced
1 stick celery, chopped
12 oz (350 g) lentils, washed
  and drained

3¼ pt (2 l) water or stock
1 teaspoon ground cumin
½ teaspoon dried thyme
1 bay leaf
juice of 1 lemon (optional)
salt and black pepper to taste

Heat the oil or butter in a heavy saucepan and sauté the onion and garlic until well softened. Add the carrot and celery, stir well, cover and sauté a further 5 minutes. Add the lentils, water or stock, cumin powder, thyme and bay leaf. Bring to the boil, reduce heat, cover and simmer for 1 hour. Add the lemon juice (if used) and season to taste with salt and black pepper. If you want a smooth soup, blend and reheat before serving.

Recipe 2

3¼ pt (2 l) water or stock
12 oz (350 g) lentils, washed
  and drained
½ teaspoon dill seeds, crushed
  (optional)
1 bunch parsley, chopped fine

2 oz (50 g) butter
1 large onion, sliced in rings
1 clove garlic, crushed
1 teaspoon paprika
salt and black pepper to taste

Put the water and lentils in a heavy pan, bring to the boil, reduce heat, cover and simmer for 30 minutes. Add the parsley and dill seeds and cook a further 45 minutes or until the lentils are very soft. Meanwhile, melt the butter in a heavy frying pan, add the onion, garlic and paprika, and sauté until the onion is well softened. Just before the soup is cooked, stir the contents of the frying pan into it and season to taste with salt and black pepper. Cook a further 5 minutes and then serve.

Cream of almond soup

A lovely soup, excellent as a first course to an exotic dinner!

8 oz (225 g) almonds
1 teaspoon coriander seeds
8 fl oz (225 ml) milk
1½ pt (800 ml) vegetable stock
  or water

2 oz (50g) fine breadcrumbs
salt and black pepper to taste
8 fl oz (225 ml) single cream

Combine the almonds and coriander seeds and pass them through a fine grinder, crush them together in a pestle and mortar, or use an electric coffee grinder. Put the milk, stock, breadcrumbs arfd almond/coriander mixture into a heavy pot and gently bring to the boil. Reduce heat, cover and simmer for 10 to 15 minutes. Remove from the heat, season to taste with salt and black pepper, stir in the cream and then gently reheat but do not allow the soup to boil. Adjust seasoning and serve.

Dried fruit soup

This is a nourishing colourful winter soup which can be served as a meal on its own.

1 medium onion, diced
2 oz (50 g) butter or vegetable oil
4 oz (100 g) chick peas (or red beans) soaked overnight and drained
4 oz (100 g) lentils, washed and drained
¼ teaspoon turmeric
¼ teaspoon ground cinnamon
¼ teaspoon ground cardamom

¼ teaspoon ground cumin
3¼ pt (2 l) water or stock
8 oz (225 g) mixed chopped dried fruit (e.g. apricots, prunes, pears, apples, etc.)
2 oz (50 g) chopped walnuts
salt and black pepper to taste
juice of 1 lemon
2 tablespoons chopped parsley or mint

Sauté the onion in the butter in a heavy pan until well softened. Stir in the lentils, chick peas and spices and mix well. Add the water or stock, bring to the boil, reduce heat, cover and simmer for 1 hour or until the chick peas are cooked. Add the dried fruit and walnuts and season to taste with salt and black pepper. Leave to cook for a further 20 minutes. Stir in the lemon juice, adjust the seasoning and serve garnished with parsley or mint. For variation in colour, add one peeled and diced beetroot to the soup at the same time as the water.

Yoghurt soups

Yoghurt is often used in Middle Eastern soups both as a thickening agent and for its own distinctive flavour. To prevent the yoghurt curdling it is either added at the end of the cooking time, after whcih the soup is not allowed to come to the boil again, or it is stabilized by slow cooking with flour and egg before addition to the soup.

Chilled yoghurt soups, which are prepared cold, have no curdling problems.

For soup making it will probably be more economical and the soup will taste better if you prepare your own yoghurt (see p. 28).

Hot yoghurt soup

4 oz (100 g) barley, washed
16 fl oz (450 ml) water
2 oz (50 g) butter
1 medium onion, finely
  chopped
1 pt (575 ml) yoghurt
1 egg

1 tablespoon cornflour
1¼ pt (700 ml) stock or water
salt and black pepper to taste
2 tablespoons crushed dried
  mint *or*
5 tablespoons chopped fresh
  mint

Cook the barley in the 16 fl oz (450 ml) water until soft and tender (about 1 hour). Fry the onion in half the butter until brown, and set aside. Gently heat the yoghurt in a heavy pan and carefully beat in the egg. Mix the cornflour into a smooth paste with a little of the 1¼ pt (700 ml) stock and whisk this into the egg and yoghurt. Stirring all the time, add the remainder of the stock to the yoghurt and slowly bring the mixture to the boil. Reduce the heat to as low as possible and add the fried onion and the cooked barley. Season to taste with salt and black pepper and leave to simmer while you prepare the mint. Melt the remaining butter in the frying pan and sauté the dried or fresh mint for 2 to 3 minutes. Stir the butter and mint into the soup and serve.

Fresh coriander or parsley may be used instead of mint, and the barley can be replaced by rice or one of the pulses such as chick peas or lentils. Other variations include using a leek in place of the onion and/or adding 1 or 2 cloves of crushed garlic along with the egg in the yoghurt.

Armenian yoghurt and noodle soup

2 oz (50 g) butter
1 medium onion, finely
  chopped
2 tablespoons dried mint
2 pt (1 l) water or stock

4 oz (100 g) egg noodles or
  other small pasta
salt and black pepper to taste
1 egg, beaten
1 pt (575 ml) yoghurt

Fry the onion in the butter until golden brown. Stir in the mint and set aside. Put the water and noodles in a heavy pot and bring to the boil. Reduce the heat and simmer until the noodles are just tender. Meanwhile whisk the beaten egg into the yoghurt and then carefully stir in some of the water in which the noodles are cooking. Slowly stir the mixture back into the noodles and continue cooking gently and stirring. When the noodles are tender, add the mint, onion and butter mixture. Heat, stirring, for a further minute or two and then serve.

To add extra flavour to the soup beat 2 cloves of crushed garlic into the yoghurt before adding it to the noodles.

Chilled soups

Cucumber and yoghurt soup

1 medium cucumber, peeled
  and finely chopped
1½ pt (850 ml) yoghurt
10 fl oz (275 ml) cold water
2 oz (50 g) dried fruit, washed,
  soaked and chopped
  (optional)

1 tablespoon finely chopped
  fresh mint or parsley
juice of ½ a lemon
1 clove garlic, finely chopped
salt and black pepper to taste

Salt the cucumber slices, reserving a few for decoration, and leave in a colander for 30 minutes. Rinse and drain. Beat the yoghurt and water together. Add most of the cucumber and the remaining ingredients. Chill well and serve garnished with the reserved cucumber.

Avocado soup

2 oz (50 g) butter
1 in (2.5 cm) piece ginger root,
  peeled and thinly sliced
2 oz (50 g) flour
1 pt (575 ml) milk

peel of ½ a lemon, grated
2 medium avocados, stoned and
  skinned
8 fl oz (225 ml) cream
salt to taste

Melt the butter in a heavy saucepan and sauté the ginger root over gentle heat for 5 minutes. Stir in the flour to form a smooth mixture and cook for 2 to 3 minutes. Slowly beat in the milk, add the lemon peel and cook the sauce over low heat, stirring, for a further 10 minutes. Remove the sauce from the heat. Leave to cool a little and then blend it with the avocado flesh. Season to taste with salt, and if the soup is too thick add more milk. Pour the soup into a large bowl, stir in the cream and leave to chill before serving.

Israeli fruit soup

A very refreshing soup and a lovely starter to a summer meal. The fruits given in the recipe are just suggestions and different combinations according to the season can be used. In winter this soup can be served hot, accompanied by a bowl of buttered boiled potatoes.

2 medium apples (cooking
  apples or Granny Smiths are
  the best), peeled, cored and
  sliced
1 peach, stoned and sliced
1 large or 2 small pears, peeled,
  cored and sliced
8 oz (225 g) plums, stoned
8 oz (225 g) apricots, stoned
2 oz (50 g) cherries or grapes,
  stoned

2 in (5 cm) stick cinnamon
4 whole cloves, stuck into a
  piece of fruit
juice of ½ a lemon
3 pt (1.75 l) water
sugar to taste
1 tablespoon cornflour in 3
  tablespoons water

Put all the contents except the cornflour paste into a heavy saucepan and bring to the boil. Remove any foam, reduce heat, cover and gently simmer for 20 minutes or until the fruits are tender. Remove the cinnamon stick and cloves. The soup can now be put through a sieve or blender, or the fruit can be left as it is, in pieces. Whichever method is preferred, now stir in the cornflour paste and cook the soup, stirring, until it thickens. Allow to cool, chill and serve.

SALADS AND PICKLES

Salads are served at every meal including breakfast. They can be composed of raw or cooked vegetables, pulses, bulgar wheat, fruit, nuts or olives in any combination, always liberally dressed with olive oil and lemon seasoned with a little salt and maybe a sprig of parsley.

For uncooked salads choose fresh, crisp vegetables or lettuce. When vegetables are cooked for salads they should be slightly underdone so that they retain their shape and texture. Pulses should be cooked to just before the point when they start to crumble, unless they are to be puréed.

The most popular salads in the Middle East are usually some combination of cucumber, tomatoes, onion, lettuce, red and green peppers and olives, all of which are plentiful and cheap during most of the year. When making a salad dressing remember the traditional advice that it needs four men to make a good dressing: 'A generous man to add the oil, a mean man to add the lemon juice, a wise man to add the salt and a fool to toss it!' Cooked foods are best dressed still warm, when they will absorb the dressing better.

In a hot climate pickling is an important method of preserving food, and even with modern conveniences such as refrigeration pickles are still an important part of the Middle Eastern larder. Pickles are served as *mezze*, with a salad, or to accompany a main meal. Most vegetables can be pickled although mixed vegetables, aubergines and turnips are particularly popular. The pickling agent generally used is a salty vinegar solution.

Popular Middle Eastern salads

Salads of lettuce, cucumber, tomatoes and onion are popular every-
where in the Middle East. The quantity of each ingredient used and
the way in which they are combined depends on personal choice
and local tradition. Below are three suggested combinations: each
uses the same basic oil and lemon dressing, while the last one is
made extra spicy by the addition of chilli pepper. To make the salads
more substantial add cubes of feta cheese and olives.

Recipe 1

1 small lettuce, shredded by
  hand
1 cucumber, thinly sliced
2 tomatoes, quartered
1 bunch spring onions, chopped
1 medium mild onion, diced

1 bunch parsley, chopped
2 tablespoons fresh mint,
  chopped, *or*
1 teaspoon dried mint
1 clove garlic

Dressing
2 fl oz (50 ml) olive oil or other
  vegetable oil

3 tablespoons lemon juice
salt and black pepper to taste

Wash and prepare all the vegetables, the parsley and the mint. Rub
the inside of a large bowl with the clove of garlic. Combine the
ingredients of the dressing and add the clove of garlic, crushed. Mix
well. Put the vegetables into the bowl, mix well, toss with the
dressing and serve.

Recipe 2

½ medium cucumber, peeled
  and cubed
1 medium, mild onion, halved
  and sliced
4 large tomatoes, chopped
1 green pepper, seeded, cored
  and diced

small bunch watercress,
  chopped
2 tablespoons fresh dill,
  chopped (optional), *or*
1 teaspoon dried dill (optional)

Dressing
2 fl oz (50 ml) olive oil or other
  vegetable oil
3 tablespoons lemon juice

2 cloves garlic, crushed
salt and black pepper to taste

Combine the vegetables and dill, if used, in a large bowl and mix
well. Mix the dressing, pour over the salad, toss well and serve.

Recipe 3

1 small cucumber, cubed
1 medium onion, diced
2 large tomatoes, chopped
1 small lettuce, shredded by hand
1 tablespoon fresh parsley, chopped
1 tablespoon fresh mint, chopped (optional)

2 fl oz (50 ml) olive oil or other vegetable oil
juice of 1 medium lemon
1 chilli pepper, finely chopped, *or*
½ to 1 teaspoon hot pepper sauce
salt and black pepper to taste

Combine all the ingredients, mix well and serve.

Orange and onion salad

2 large, sweet oranges
2 medium onions, thinly sliced
black olives, halved and stoned

3 tablespoons olive oil or other vegetable oil
juice of 1 lemon

For this Turkish salad peel the oranges, being careful to remove all the white pith, and slice them crosswise into rings. In a bowl arrange alternate layers of onion and orange. Garnish the top with olives. Combine the olive oil and lemon juice and pour over.

Orange and avocado salad

This Israeli salad is like the recipe above, but substitute cubes of avocado flesh for the onions and cut the orange slices into small pieces.

Beetroot salad

Either use pre-cooked beetroots, or use fresh ones and boil them as described in the recipe. Two salad dressings to choose from are given. The first is an oil, lemon juice and garlic combination which is a big improvement on the sharp vinegar dressing usually associated with beetroot. The second uses yoghurt as a main ingredient and the colour and tang of natural yoghurt contrast well with the colour and taste of the beetroot.

1 lb (450 g) uncooked beetroots

Oil and lemon dressing
2 fl oz (50 ml) vegetable oil
2 tablespoons lemon juice
2 cloves garlic, crushed
2 tablespoons chopped fresh
  parsley
salt and black pepper to taste

Yoghurt dressing
8 fl oz (225 ml) yoghurt
2 cloves garlic, crushed
1 teaspoon caraway seeds
salt and black pepper to taste
paprika for garnishing

Leave the beetroots whole and unpeeled. Scrub them and then boil them in plenty of salty water for 1 to 2 hours, depending on size, until they are tender. Drain, rub off the skins and slice them. Set the slices aside in a bowl.

Prepare either of the dressings by combining the ingredients and mixing well. Pour the chosen dressing over the sliced beetroots and serve. If you are making the yoghurt dressing garnish the bowl with a pinch of paprika.

Israeli breakfast salad

The kibbutz breakfast has become well known in Israel and is served in hotels as an English or Continental breakfast may be served in the West. A selection of fresh vegetables cleaned but left whole (although you may of course pre-chop them if you wish) is arranged on a large plate and served with a variety of salad dressing ingredients. Each person at the table creates his own combination of salad vegetable and dressing.

Wash, dry and chill a selection of vegetables, e.g.

tomatoes
green and red peppers
cabbage, shredded
lettuce, shredded
cucumbers
carrots

celery
radishes
onion, cut in rings
olives
fresh parsley, chopped

Provide small bowls of:
olive or other vegetable oil
yoghurt
sour cream
olive oil with garlic, crushed

vinegar
lemon, quartered
salt and black pepper

Provide each person with a plate, sharp knife, and a small bowl in which to mix their own salad dressing. Serve with warm pitta bread or other fresh bread.

Cooked green pepper salad

Green peppers are usually used fresh in salads but sometimes they are cooked first, chilled and then served as a side salad.

4 medium green peppers	2 tablespoons vegetable oil
2 fl oz (50 ml) lemon juice or good vinegar	2 cloves garlic, crushed
	salt and black pepper to taste

Preheat the oven to 400° F (205° C, gas mark 6). Place the peppers on a greased flat baking tray and roast them for 20 minutes, turning them a few times. Remove them from the oven, peel off the skin, halve them, remove the core and seeds and cut them in strips. Mix together the lemon juice or vinegar, oil and garlic, season to taste with salt and black pepper, and pour this dressing over the peppers. Chill and serve.

An alternative method is to sauté the cooked pepper strips in a little butter or oil for 2 to 3 minutes, season them with salt only and serve hot.

Cooked green pepper and tomato salad

4 medium green peppers	3 tablespoons lemon juice
4 firm tomatoes	3 tablespoons vegetable oil
1 clove garlic, crushed	salt to taste
1 teaspoon cumin seeds	
¼ teaspoon hot pepper sauce or chopped chilli pepper	

Prepare cooked green pepper strips as described in the recipe above. Plunge the tomatoes into boiling water for 2 minutes and then chill immediately in cold water. Skin and chop them. Put the peppers and tomatoes together in a bowl. Combine the remaining ingredients and pour the mixture over the peppers and tomatoes. Place in the refrigerator for 20 to 30 minutes and then serve.

Tomato salad

If possible use large, firm, tasty tomatoes. For a simple salad slice the tomatoes, arrange them on a plate with some black or green olives, dress with olive oil, lemon juice, salt and pepper, garnish with chopped fresh parsley, and serve. For a slightly more substantial salad use the following recipe.

1 large onion, finely diced
1 lb (450 g) large, firm
  tomatoes, chopped
1 medium green pepper,
  seeded, cored and sliced

1 bunch fresh parsley, chopped
salt, vegetable oil and vinegar
  or lemon juice to taste

Salt the onion pieces and set aside under a weight for 20 to 30 minutes. Rinse well under cold water and drain. Combine with the tomatoes, green pepper and parsley and dress to taste with salt, oil and vinegar or lemon.

Simple carrot salad

4 medium carrots, peeled and
  grated
2 oz (50 g) raisins, soaked and
  drained

2 fl oz (50 ml) fresh or canned
  orange juice

Combine the ingredients, chill and serve. Add a little sugar for a sweeter salad or a pinch of salt for a more savoury one.

Moroccan carrot salad

This is a slightly complicated recipe but the result gives the humble carrot an exotic new taste. Make more than you need since the salad will keep for over a week if refrigerated.

1 lb (450 g) medium carrots,
  peeled and sliced
1 pt (450 ml) water
1 teaspoon salt
4 cloves garlic, crushed
½ bunch fresh parsley, finely
  chopped

1 teaspoon salt
1 teaspoon ground cumin
½ teaspoon hot pepper sauce
  or chopped chilli pepper
2 fl oz (50 ml) vegetable oil
3 tablespoons lemon juice or
  vinegar

Put the carrots, water and salt in a pot and bring to the boil. Reduce heat and simmer until the carrots are not quite tender. Remove from the heat and set the pot and its contents aside. Pound the garlic, parsley, salt, cumin powder and hot pepper sauce or chopped chilli pepper into a paste. Heat the vegetable oil in a small, heavy frying pan, mix in the paste and carefully add 8 fl oz (225 ml) of the water the carrots were cooked in. Bring the mixture to the boil, stirring, and then pour it into the pot with the carrots and the remaining cooking water. Stir in the lemon juice or vinegar. Transfer the carrots and liquid to a bowl or storage jar, chill and serve.

Cabbage and tangerine salad

This unusual combination is a Turkish invention.

½ small white cabbage, finely
  shredded
1 to 2 tangerines, peeled and
  sliced

juice of 1 lemon
salt and oil to taste

Combine the shredded cabbage and tangerine slices, and sprinkle over the lemon juice and salt. Mix well, pour over vegetable oil to taste and serve.

Potato salad

1 lb (450 g) new potatoes,
  scrubbed clean
2 large tomatoes, quartered and
  then halved
juice of 1 lemon

2 cloves garlic, crushed
3 tablespoons olive oil
salt and black pepper to taste
few sprigs fresh parsley or mint
  leaves for garnishing

Boil the potatoes until just tender. Drain and allow them to cool a little. Cut the potatoes into quarters and combine them with the tomatoes, being careful not to crush either vegetable. Mix the lemon juice, oil, garlic and salt and pepper together, pour over the potatoes and tomatoes and garnish with parsley or mint.

Alternatively you may leave the tomatoes out and substitute finely diced onion, leek or spring onion.

Potato and egg salad

1 lb (450 g) new potatoes,
  scrubbed clean
4 eggs, hard-boiled, shelled and
  sliced
1 small onion, finely sliced

juice of 1 lemon
3 tablespoons olive oil
salt to taste
sprigs of parsley for garnishing

Boil the potatoes until just tender. Drain, cool a little and then cut them into thick slices. Arrange in a bowl alternate layers of sliced potatoes, eggs and onion. Combine the lemon juice, oil and salt and pour over. Garnish with parsley and serve.

Middle Eastern egg and vegetable salad

This traditional cooked salad can also be served as a first or main course dish.

2 tablespoons vegetable oil
1 lb (450 g) tomatoes, sliced
2 medium green peppers,
  seeded, cored and cut into
  strips

1 chilli pepper, finely diced
3 cloves garlic, crushed
salt to taste
8 medium or small eggs

Preheat the oven to 350° F (175° C, gas mark 4). Heat the oil in a heavy pan, add the tomatoes, green peppers, chilli pepper, garlic and salt to taste. Sauté over a low heat until the vegetables are just cooked. Cover the base of a baking dish with the mixture and carefully break in the 8 eggs. Keep the eggs separate from one another. Bake in the oven for 10 minutes or until the eggs are well set. Serve. The usual serving is 2 eggs per person.

Avocado salad

The Israelis add avocado to advantage to almost any salad. Here is just one example.

2 medium ripe but firm
  avocados, peeled
2 medium tomatoes, sliced
¼ medium cucumber, sliced
2 eggs, hard-boiled, shelled and
  quartered

juice of 1 lemon
2 tablespoons vegetable oil
salt and black pepper to taste

Cut the avocados in half and remove the stones. Slice vertically and then crosswise. Combine the avacado pieces with the tomatoes, cucumber and egg. Mix the oil and lemon juice together, season to taste with salt and black pepper and pour the dressing over the salad.

Globe artichoke salad

4 medium globe artichokes,
  rinsed
4 tablespoons vegetable oil
1 clove garlic, crushed
1 tablespoon lemon juice or
  vinegar

3 tablespoons yoghurt
  (optional)
salt to taste

Choose artichokes with firm, moist leaves, and put them in a large pan of water. Bring to the boil and simmer for 20 to 25 minutes or until a leaf can easily be pulled off. Drain and cool. Combine the remaining ingredients, mix well, and, put this dressing in a bowl.

Serve each person with an artichoke. Take the leaves off one at a time, dip the fleshy end in the dressing and then gently scrape the flesh off between your teeth. Repeat until you reach the prickly centre or choke, as it is called. Scrape the choke away and the heart will be revealed; cut this away from the stalk and dip it in the dressing before eating.

Tabbouleh (bulgar wheat salad)

This Lebanese and Syrian salad is perhaps one of the best-known Middle Eastern salads. It's easy to prepare and has a fresh, tangy taste. There are many variations on the basic recipe but they always contain plenty of fresh parsley and lemon juice.

8 oz (225 g) fine bulgar wheat (cracked wheat will do)

8 oz (225 g) onion or spring onions, finely chopped

8 oz (125 g) fresh parsley, chopped

4 tablespoons fresh mint leaves, chopped, *or*

4 teaspoons crushed dried mint

3 medium tomatoes, finely chopped

4 fl oz (100 ml) lemon juice

4 fl oz (100 ml) olive oil

salt and black pepper to taste

1 fresh lettuce, washed and separated into leaves

Cover the bulgar wheat in plenty of cold water and leave for 1 hour. Drain and squeeze out any excess water. Put the swollen wheat into a large bowl and gently stir in all the remaining ingredients except the lettuce leaves. Taste, and adjust the seasoning. Cover the surface of a large serving dish with a few lettuce leaves, pile on the *tabbouleh* and surround it with the remaining lettuce leaves which are then used to scoop up the salad.

If you add other ingredients to the salad be careful not to lose the fresh lemon taste which is an essential quality of *tabbouleh*.

Cucumber in yoghurt (cacik)

This salad, of Turkish or Greek origin, is now a great favourite all over the Middle East. It can be served as a salad, as a garnish for soup, or as a side dish to a main meal. See p. 23 in the chapter on *mezze* for a different *cacik* recipe.

1 medium cucumber, peeled
　and thinly sliced
4 radishes, finely sliced
1 tablespoon chopped chives or
　spring onions

pinch of salt
8 fl oz (225 ml) yoghurt
few sprigs fresh mint for
　garnish

Combine the cucumber, radishes and chives, add a pinch of salt, and pour on the yoghurt. Chill, garnish with mint and serve. One clove of garlic, finely chopped, may be added to the salad if you wish, and sometimes a few drops of vinegar and olive oil are stirred in.

Cucumber relish

This is a Moroccan salad in which the ingredients are very finely sliced and marinated in oil and vinegar. The ingredients include 2 chilli peppers and consequently the salad is very hot.

1 medium cucumber, peeled
　and diced into ¼ in (1.3 cm)
　cubes
1 large, firm tomato, finely
　chopped

1 small onion, finely diced
2 chilli peppers, finely diced
3 tablespoons vegetable oil
2 tablespoons vinegar
salt to taste

Combine all the ingredients and leave to marinate for 1 hour. For a milder salad use only 1 chilli pepper.

Pilaki (cooked vegetable salad)

Pilaki is a great favourite in Turkey, where the salad is served cold as a side dish to main meals. It improves with keeping. The recipe as given may be too oily for some tastes, in which case use only half or a quarter of the quantity of oil given.

6 fl oz (175 ml) vegetable oil
2 medium onions, quartered
4 medium tomatoes, quartered
4 medium green peppers,
　seeded, cored and cut into
　strips

½ teaspoon cumin seeds
½ teaspoon hot pepper sauce
salt to taste
6 fl oz (175 ml) water

Heat the oil in a frying pan, then add all the ingredients except the water. Sir and sauté for 3 to 4 minutes. Add the water slowly, reduce the heat and simmer until all the vegetables are soft (about 15 minutes). Allow to cool before serving.

Aubergine salads

To prepare aubergines for salad making, impale them on a skewer or fork and gently toast them all over, over a gas flame or electric plate or under a grill, until all the skin is blackened and the inside feels soft and mushy. For larger aubergines, lightly oil the skins and place them on a low shelf in an oven at 350° F (175° C, gas mark 4) for about 1 hour or until cooked right through.

Slice open the prepared aubergines and scoop out all the flesh. Squeeze some lemon juice over it to prevent discoloration, and leave the flesh to drain in a colander.

Syrian aubergine salad

1 large or 2 medium aubergines, prepared as above
1 medium onion, finely diced
1 small bunch fresh parsley, chopped
2 tablespoons vinegar
2 fl oz (50 ml) vegetable oil
salt and black pepper to taste
2 medium tomatoes, quartered
sprigs of mint for garnish (optional)

Chop the aubergine flesh into small pieces and combine it with the onion and parsley. Mix together the vinegar, oil and seasoning. Pour this dressing over the aubergine and onion mixture and chill. Serve the salad garnished with tomato and sprigs of mint, if liked.

Turkish aubergine salad

1 large or 2 medium aubergines, prepared as above
2 fl oz (50 ml) vegetable oil
2 fl oz (50 ml) yoghurt
1 clove garlic, crushed
salt to taste
2 tomatoes, cut in eighths
1 medium green pepper, seeded, cored and cut in strips
½ medium onion, sliced
black or green olives for garnishing

Put the aubergine pulp, oil, yoghurt and garlic in a bowl and beat the mixture into a smooth cream. Season to taste with salt and chill. Pour the chilled aubergine cream on to a dish, and surround it with tomato, green pepper and onion. Garnish with olives and serve with bread.

Lebanese aubergine salad

1 large or 2 medium
  aubergines, prepared as above
3 tablespoons tahini
juice of 1 lemon
2 cloves of garlic, crushed
salt to taste

¼ teaspoon hot pepper sauce
  (optional)
olive oil to taste
sprigs of parsley for garnishing
1 medium green pepper, seeded
  and sliced, for garnishing

Chop the aubergine pulp into small pieces. Stir in the tahini, lemon juice and garlic. Season to taste with salt. Place the mixture on a serving dish, pour over olive oil to taste, and garnish with sprigs of parsley and rings of green pepper. For a touch of spice add ¼ teaspoon of hot pepper sauce to the ingredients. Serve with bread and young lettuce leaves.

Chick pea and bulgar wheat salad

8 oz (225 g) chick peas, soaked
  overnight and drained
2 tablespoons vegetable oil
1 small onion, diced
4 oz (100 g) bulgar wheat

4 oz (100 g) tomato paste
salt and black pepper to taste
2 tablespoons chopped fresh
  parsley for garnishing

Cook the chick peas in plenty of water until just tender. Drain and reserve liquid for use in soups, etc. Put the oil in a heavy pan, add the onion and sauté until golden. Add the chick peas, bulgar wheat and tomato paste, mix well and stir in 8 fl oz (225 ml) of the reserved liquid. Season to taste with salt and black pepper and leave to simmer for 20 minutes. Add a little extra water if it dries out. Turn the hot salad into a serving bowl and chill. Garnish with parsley and serve. The salad may also be served hot as a side dish.

Turkish white bean salad

8 oz (225 gm) haricot beans,
  soaked overnight and drained
1 medium onion, thinly sliced
1 egg, hard–boiled, shelled and
  sliced
2 medium tomatoes, sliced

12 black olives, halved and
  stoned
juice of 1 lemon
2 tablespoons olive oil
2 to 3 sprigs fresh parsley for
  garnishing

Cook the beans in plenty of water until just tender. Drain and reserve the cooking liquid for future use in soups, etc. Leave the beans to cool and then pour them into a serving bowl. Cover them with sliced onion, egg and tomatoes, decorate with olives and pour over the lemon juice and oil. Garnish with parsley and serve.

Spinach salad

1 lb (450 gm) spinach, washed and chopped
1 medium onion, finely diced
1 tablespoon olive oil
8 fl oz (225 ml) yoghurt

1 clove garlic, finely chopped
2 tablespoons chopped walnuts
1 teaspoon crushed dried mint for garnishing

Put the spinach and onion in a heavy pan. Cover and gently cook, with no added water, until the spinach is wilted and soft (about 10 minutes). Add the oil and cook a further 5 minutes. Combine the yoghurt and garlic and lightly toast the walnuts. Transfer the spinach and onion to a serving bowl, pour over the yoghurt, sprinkle over the walnuts, garnish with crushed mint and serve hot.

Lentil salad

12 oz (350 gm) green or brown lentils, washed
1 medium onion, whole
2 cloves
2 bay leaves
2 cloves garlic
1 teaspoon grated lemon peel

1 medium onion, diced
2 tablespoons vegetable oil
2 tablespoons lemon juice
½ teaspoon ground cumin
½ teaspoon ground coriander
salt and black pepper to taste
olives for garnishing

Put the lentils in a heavy pot and cover them with water. Stick the cloves in the onion and add it to the pot. Add the bay leaves, whole garlic cloves and lemon rind. Bring to the boil, reduce heat, cover and simmer until the lentils are just tender (not disintegrating). Drain the lentils; separate the onion and cloves, bay leaves and garlic and discard them. Combine the lentils with the remaining ingredients, except for the olives, and set the salad aside to chill and marinate for 1 to 2 hours. Garnish with the olives and serve.

Egyptian ful bean salad

8 oz (225 gm) *ful* beans, soaked
   overnight and drained
4 cloves garlic, crushed
½ teaspoon salt
juice of 1 lemon
1 small onion, diced
1 tablespoon chopped fresh
   parsley for garnishing
1 tablespoon chopped fresh
   mint, *or*
½ teaspoon crushed dried
   mint, for garnishing
2 fl oz (50 ml) olive oil

Cook the beans in plenty of water until tender. Drain and reserve the liquid for future use in soups, etc. Put the beans in a bowl. Crush the salt and garlic together and stir into the beans. Add the lemon juice and diced onion and mix well. Garnish with parsley and mint and pour over the oil.

Green bean salad

1 lb (450 g) green beans,
   washed and cut into 2 in
   (5 cm) pieces
1 medium onion, finely sliced
2 medium tomatoes, quartered

1 bunch parsley, chopped
2 tablespoons vinegar or lemon
   juice
2 fl oz (50 ml) olive oil
salt to taste

Drop the beans into a pan of boiling, salted water and simmer until they are just tender. Drain, and cool them under running cold water. Combine the cooked beans with the remaining ingredients, gently mix and serve.

Pickles

Vegetables were originally pickled to preserve them for times of scarcity, but nowadays refrigeration has made this unnecessary and pickles are prepared and valued more for their own taste and texture than as preserves. A feature of Middle Eastern life, they are sold in restaurants and market places and made in many homes.

Raw or lightly cooked vegetables are left to soak in a salty vinegar solution in airtight jars. The amount of salt and vinegar used is a question of personal choice, but there must be enough of each or the solution loses its preserving qualities.

Generally, the stronger the solution the longer the vegetables will keep. In some of the recipes given below the amounts of vinegar, water and salt required are detailed, but for general purposes the following recipe makes a good all-round pickling solution.

General pickling solution

2 pt (1 l) water
12 fl oz (350 ml) vinegar (malt,
    cider or white wine)
3 oz (75 g) salt

Combine the ingredients and stir well, warming if necessary, until the salt is dissolved. For sweeter pickles add 1 tablespoon of sugar.

Turkish mixed pickles

1 lb (450 g) tomatoes
1 lb (450 g) small pickling
cucumbers, cleaned
1 lb (450 g) green peppers,
seeded and cleaned

4 cloves garlic
vinegar
salt

Plunge the tomatoes into boiling water for 1 to 2 minutes, then submerge them in cold water and remove the skins. Cut the peppers into thick strips. Pack the vegetables tightly into clean pickling jars in an attractive pattern and place 1 or 2 cloves of garlic in each jar. Sprinkle 1 teaspoon of salt per 12 oz (350 g) of vegetables into each jar and pour in vinegar to the brim. Seal tightly and store in a cool place. They will be ready in 2 to 4 weeks.

Armenian mixed pickles

4 large carrots, cleaned
1 small cauliflower, separated
into small florets
8 oz (225 g) green beans, cut
into 4 in (10 cm) pieces, *or*
1 medium green pepper,
seeded, cored and cut in thick
strips

2 cloves garlic
2 teaspoons dill seeds
general pickling solution (see
above)

Quarter the carrots lengthwise and cut each piece in half. Pack the vegetables tightly and attractively into clean pickling jars. Add a clove or part of a clove of garlic, and a proportion of dill seeds, to each jar. Combine the ingredients for the pickling solution and bring the solution to the boil. Pour this solution into the packed jars and seal tightly. Store in a cool place. The pickles will be ready in 2 to 4 weeks. The longer you leave them the sharper the taste will become. They are good for up to 2 months or longer if refrigerated.

Pickled turnips

Surprisingly perhaps, pickled turnips are one of the favourite Middle Eastern pickles. They are normally coloured by slices of raw or lightly cooked beetroot added to the pickling jar. They have a pleasing, individual flavour.

1 medium beetroot, peeled,
washed and sliced thinly
2 lb (900 g) small white turnips,
peeled and washed

2 cloves garlic
3 to 4 sprigs celery leaves
general pickling solution (see
above)

Cut the turnips into halves, or if they are rather large into quarters, and pack them tightly into cleaned pickling jars, placing a slice of beetroot between each piece of turnip. Add a clove or part of a clove of garlic and a sprig of celery to each jar. Cover the vegetables with pickling solution and seal tightly. Store in a cool place; the pickles will be ready in about 2 weeks. Do not keep for longer than 6 weeks unless refrigerated.

Pickled aubergines

2 lb (900 g) small aubergines
1 stick celery, cleaned and cut
into 1 in (2.5 cm) pieces
4 oz (100 g) carrots, cleaned
and cut into 1 in (2.5 cm)
pieces
2 chilli peppers, seeded and
finely chopped

4 cloves garlic
3 to 4 sprigs celery leaves
1 pt (575 ml) water
1 pt (575 ml) cider or white
wine vinegar
3 tablespoons salt

Make a small cut in the side of each aubergine. Part boil the aubergines whole in a pan of salted boiling water for 5 to 10 minutes. Drain and carefully squeeze out as much water as possible. Cut them into quarters, pack the pieces into clean pickling jars and distribute equal portions of carrot, celery, chilli peppers, garlic and celery leaves between each jar. Combine the water and vinegar and dissolve the salt in the mixture. Pour this solution over the aubergines right up to the brims of the jars and seal tightly. Store in a cool place. They will be ready in about 2 weeks or a little longer, and are good for around 5 months or more if kept under refrigeration.

Chopped walnuts – about 2 oz (50 g) per 1 lb (450 g) of aubergines – are sometimes added to this pickle.

Pickled cucumbers

2 lb (900 g) small pickling
cucumbers, cleaned
½ medium onion, finely sliced
6 peppercorns
1 teaspoon coriander seeds
1 teaspoon dill seeds

1 bay leaf, crumbled
1 pt (575 ml) water
16 fl oz (450 ml) white wine
vinegar
2 tablespoons salt

Pack the cucumbers tightly in clean pickling jars, distributing the peppercorns, coriander and dill seeds, bay leaf and onion slices evenly between them. Combine the water, vinegar and salt and stir until the salt is dissolved. Pour the solution over the cucumbers up to the brims of the jars. Seal tightly and store in a warm place for 10 days, when they will be ready to eat. The pickles will keep up to 6 weeks without refrigeration.

Sweet pickled grapes

1 lb (450 g) seedless grapes, washed
4 fl oz (100 ml) white wine vinegar
4 fl oz (100 ml) water
juice of 1 large orange

3 in (7.5 cm) stick cinnamon
2 cloves
1 tablespoon sugar

Remove the grapes from the stalks and pull out any stems. Combine the remaining ingredients and bring to the boil. Set aside to cool. Remove the cinnamon stick. Pack the grapes into a clean pickling jar and pour the solution over them. Seal tightly and leave for 2 days. They are now ready and will keep up to 2 weeks.

Dried apricot pickle

1 lb (450 g) dried apricots
1 in (2.5 cm) piece of ginger root, peeled and finely chopped
1½ pt (¾ to 1 l) vinegar (malt, cider or white wine variety)

2 tablespoons coriander seeds
4 oz (100 g) sugar
¼ teaspoon cayenne
1 bulb of garlic, all cloves peeled
1 teaspoon salt
½ teaspoon black pepper

For this very spicy Iranian pickle, soak the apricots and ginger in the vinegar for 4 to 6 hours. Put the apricots, ginger and vinegar in a heavy pan, then add the coriander seeds and the remaining ingredients. Bring the mixture to the boil, reduce the heat and simmer uncovered until the mixture is thickened. Pour the contents of the pan into clean jars and seal tightly. The pickled apricots are ready for use after 1 week. They will keep up to 6 weeks.

BREADS AND SAVOURY BISCUITS

There are many varieties and shapes of Middle Eastern breads, although round, yeasted breads ranging in thickness from paper-thin to very thick are the most common. The breads are normally baked at very high temperatures for short periods of time, at home or in small local bakeries. The thin breads keep fresh for only a short time, and to provide fresh bread all the time the bakeries operate morning and evening. One of the great pleasures of being in the Middle East is to stand at a bakery door watching the baker working with such dexterity that the shaping and baking of the bread seems to take place by magic. In Iraq they use clay ovens which have been preheated with a wood fire. The dough, in large, flat rounds, is slapped against the inner surface of the oven roof where it remains stuck until baked. Just as it is about to fall off into the smouldering fire below, the baker leans in with a long iron pole, catches the bread and draws it out of the oven for the first in the line of eager customers.

Pitta bread

Pitta bread, which in one shape or another is the most common bread in the Middle East, is a soft-textured, flat, slightly leavened bread with a hollow in the middle. The rolled out dough is allowed to rise and then baked at a very high temperature for a short time; during the process the dough separates to form the pouch or hollow. Pitta bread split in half and stuffed with a filling is a popular snack food.

The following recipe makes 4 to 6 pieces of pitta bread. Strong white flour is stipulated in the recipe, since this is the type normally used, but if you wish you can substitute wholemeal flour or a softer white flour. In either case you will have to make slight adjustments to the baking times.

½ oz (12 g) fresh yeast, *or*
1 level teaspoon dried yeast
2 fl oz (50 ml) warm water
1 teaspoon sugar

1 lb (450 g) strong white flour
½ teaspoon salt
approximately 10 fl oz (275 ml)
  water

Mix the yeast, warm water and sugar into a smooth paste and set aside in a warm place for 15 to 20 minutes or until the mixture has frothed up. Combine the flour and salt in a mixing bowl and pour in the yeast mixture. Start to knead the dough by hand and slowly add enough water to form a firm dough, neither too hard nor too soft. Turn the dough on to a floured board and knead it for 10 to 15 minutes. This is vital if the bread is to have the right texture. Lightly grease a large bowl, place the dough in it and leave it covered with a damp cloth in a warm place for 1 to 1½ hours. Knead again for 2 to 3 minutes and then pinch off large, egg-size lumps. Roll each of them into ¼ in (1.3 cm) thick, 5 in (12.5 cm) diameter circles on a floured board. Dust each round with flour and set to rise again on a floured cloth in a warm place for about 20 minutes.

Meanwhile preset the oven to maximum temperature. After 10 minutes place 2 ungreased baking sheets in the oven to warm up. Lightly sprinkle the dough rounds with cold water and load them on to the hot baking sheets. Place them in the oven and bake for about 8 minutes. Do not open the oven door during this time. The finished pitta bread should be soft and white with a hollow in the middle. Serve as they are, or cut them crosswise at the middle or top and stuff with whatever filling you have ready. Store uneaten bread in plastic bags in the freezer or refrigerator. To reheat, place in a 350°F (175° C, gas mark 4) oven for about 3 minutes. Serve and eat immediately – uncovered pitta bread goes stale quickly.

The following two recipes for Lenten pies use pitta bread dough as a base.

Syrian Lenten pies

During Lent many Middle Eastern Catholics restrict themselves to a vegetarian diet. The following pies are examples of Lenten food which are delicious and can of course be made at any time of the year.

Sesame seed pies

4 oz (100 g) sesame seeds
4 oz (100 g) sugar
vegetable oil

1 lb (450 g) pitta bread dough
  (see above)

Combine the sesame seeds and sugar with enough oil to hold the mixture together. Prepare pitta bread, following the previous recipe, up to the stage when they are about to go in the oven. Spoon the sesame seed mixture on to the pitta bread rounds and then bake them in a preheated oven at 350°F (175° C, gas mark 4) for 10 minutes. Remove the pies from the oven and place them under a medium grill for 1 to 2 minutes. Serve hot or cold.

Chick pea pies

1 lb (450 g) pitta bread dough (see above)   1 lb (450 g) cooked chick peas

Prepare the pitta bread, following the recipe above, up to the stage where they are about to go in the oven. Press the chick peas on to the tops of the prepared pitta bread rounds and then bake them in a preheated oven at 350°F (175° C, gas mark 4) for 10 minutes. Remove the pies from the oven and place them under a medium grill for 2 to 3 minutes. Serve hot or cold.

Armenian round bread

Large, circular loaves made from a yeasted dough. Before baking they are brushed with melted butter.

Makes 2 loaves

1¼ lb (575 g) plain flour	2 teaspoons sugar
1 teaspoon salt	4 fl oz (100 ml) warm water
1 oz (25 g) fresh yeast, *or*	8 fl oz (225 ml) warm milk
2 teaspoons dried yeast	2 oz (50 g) melted butter

In a mixing bowl combine the salt and flour, mix well, and make a well in the centre. Dissolve the sugar in the water and crumble in the yeast. Pour this mixture, the warm milk and half the butter, melted, into the well in the flour. Knead the dough by hand for 5 minutes then cover it with a damp cloth and set it aside in a warm place for 1 hour. Knead the dough again for another few minutes and then set it aside, covered, for another hour. Now divide the dough in half and form each half into a ball shape. Roll each ball into a disc about 1 in (2.5 cm) thick and 8 to 9 in (20 to 22.5 cm) in diameter. Grease 2 baking trays and place a round of dough on each. Brush the tops with the remaining melted butter and set aside, covered, for a further hour. Preheat the oven to 375°F (190°C, gas mark 5). Bake the bread on the middle sheet for about 45 minutes. It should be firm and nicely browned when cooked.

Moroccan bread

In Morocco bread is made from wholemeal flour – it is quite heavy, but nutritious and tasty. Like other Middle Eastern breads it is baked on flat trays in large, airy ovens. Baking temperatures are quite high and cooking times short.

Makes 2 loaves

10 oz (275 g) wholemeal flour
10 oz (275 g) strong white flour
1 teaspoon salt
1 oz (25g) fresh yeast, *or*
2 teaspoons dried yeast
2 teaspoons sugar

6 fl oz (150 ml) warm milk
2 oz (50 g) melted butter
1 tablespoon anise or fennel
  seeds
½ tablespoon caraway seeds
warm water

Combine the flours and salt and mix well. Make a well in the centre. Dissolve the yeast and sugar in the milk and pour into the flour. Add the melted butter, anise or fennel seeds and caraway seeds, and stir in enough warm water to form a firm dough. Knead the dough on a floured board for 5 minutes and then form it into 2 equal-sized round balls. Grease 2 baking sheets and place a ball on each. Roll, or flatten by hand, each ball into a disc of about 8 in (20 cm) diameter. Cover each with a dampened towel and set them aside in a warm place for 2 to 3 hours or until the 2 loaves have doubled in size. Preheat oven to 450° F (230° C, gas mark 7). Bake the bread at this temperature for 10 minutes. Reduce the temperature to 350° F (175° C, gas mark 4) and bake for a further 30 minutes. Remove from the oven and cool.

Syrian loaf bread

Makes four 12 oz (350 g) loaves

1 oz (25 g) fresh yeast, *or*
2 teaspoons dried yeast
16 fl oz (450 ml) lukewarm
  water
2 oz (50 g) sugar

1½ teaspoons salt
1 tablespoon vegetable oil
2 tablespoons melted butter
1½ lb (675 g) plain strong
  white flour

This is a very slightly sweet bread. Put the water in a large mixing bowl and dissolve the yeast in it. Stir in the sugar, salt, oil and butter and mix well. Slowly beat in the flour to form a firm dough. Turn the dough on to a floured board and knead for 5 to 10 minutes or until the dough is smooth and elastic. Cover with a damp cloth and leave to rise in a warm place for 2 hours. Knead again for 2 minutes and then divide the dough into 4 equal portions. Roll each portion into a smooth ball and set them well apart on a greased baking sheet. Cover them with a damp cloth and set aside for 30 minutes in a warm place to rise. Flatten the balls with the palm of your hand to form discs about ½ in (1.3 cm) thick. Cover them with a damp cloth and leave them to rise again for 45 minutes. Preheat the oven to 450° F (230° C, gas mark 7). Bake the bread for 15 minutes or until the loaves are nicely browned on top. Remove them from the oven and cool.

Arabic wholemeal bread rounds

This bread is unyeasted and can be prepared without an oven. It is similar to the Indian chapatti.

1 lb (450 g) wholemeal flour	6 fl oz (175 ml) lukewarm
1 level teaspoon salt	water
	vegetable oil

Combine the flour and salt together and add the water. Mix well and knead into a smooth dough. The longer you knead the dough the better; 10 minutes is the minimum time required. Put the dough in a bowl, cover with a damp cloth and leave in a warm place for 2 to 3 hours. Now pinch off large egg-size pieces of dough and form them into balls. Roll them out on a lightly floured board to form rounds of about 6 in (15 cm) diameter. Cover the rounds with a dry cloth and leave for 30 minutes. Grease a heavy frying pan very lightly and heat it over a medium flame. Cook the rounds in the pan one at a time for about 1 to 2 minutes on each side or until they are nicely browned. After half of them have been cooked, re-grease the pan very lightly using a cloth dipped in oil. Store the cooked bread rounds in a warm oven or under a very low grill until needed.

Olive bread

This is a quick Turkish bread in which baking powder is used as the raising agent.

2 eggs, beaten
4 fl oz (100 ml) milk
4 fl oz (100 ml) water
1 lb (450 g) plain white flour
1 teaspoon baking powder

1 teaspoon salt
2 fl oz (50 ml) olive oil
8 oz (225 g) olives, stoned and
  chopped
1 teaspoon dried mint

Combine the eggs, milk and water. Sieve together the flour, baking powder and salt. Slowly add the liquids to this mixture to form a smooth dough. Stir in the remaining ingredients and mix well together. Preheat the oven to 350° F (175° C, gas mark 4). Grease a bread tin and spoon in the mixture. Bake for 30 minutes. Remove from the oven, turn the bread out of the tin and cool. This bread is delicious with hummus, cottage cheese, cucumber and yoghurt and many other dips and salads.

Here is an alternative method of making olive bread. Take 1 lb (450 g) of regular bread dough, and after the first rising knead into it the same amount of olive oil and chopped olives as used in the above recipe. Press the dough into a bread tin, leave to rise in a warm place for 45 minutes, and bake in a preheated oven at 350° F (175° C, gas mark 4) for 45 minutes.

Moroccan semi-sweet bread

1 lb (450 g) soft white flour
1 teaspoon salt
1 teaspoon poppy seeds
1 teaspoon caraway seeds
1 teaspoon fennel seeds

4 fl oz (100 ml) warm water
1 oz (25 g) fresh yeast, *or*
2 teaspoons dried yeast
2 tablespoons sugar

Combine the flour, salt and seeds and mix well. Dissolve the sugar and yeast in the water and stir. Add this to the flour and seed mixture, together with enough extra warm water to form a firm dough. Knead the dough for a few minutes and then pinch off large, egg-size pieces and form them into ball shapes. Press each ball into a flat disc about 3 to 4 in (7.5 to 10 cm) in diameter. Grease a baking tray (or trays) and place the dough rounds on it, leaving enough space between each for the dough to expand. Cover and set them aside in a warm place for 1 hour. Preheat the oven to 375° F (190° C, gas mark 5). Bake the dough rounds for 30 minutes or until nicely browned. Remove them from the oven and cool.

Sweet buns

Makes about 20 buns

1 lb (450 g) plain flour
½ teaspoon salt
1 teaspoon caraway seeds
2 oz (50 g) sugar
1 teaspoon ground cinnamon
½ oz (12.5 g) fresh yeast, *or*
1 teaspoon dried yeast

4 fl oz (100 ml) warm water
2 oz (50 g) melted butter
3 eggs
4 fl oz (225 ml) warm milk
sesame seeds for topping

Combine the flour, salt, caraway seeds, all the sugar except for one teaspoon, and the cinnamon powder in a large bowl and sift together. Dissolve the yeast and the teaspoonful of reserved sugar in the warm water and mix well. Make a well in the centre of the flour and pour in the yeast mixture, the melted butter, 2 of the eggs, the warm milk and enough extra (if needed) warm water to give a firm but moist dough. Knead the mixture by hand until everything is well blended. Cover the dough with a damp cloth, set aside in a warm place and leave to rise for 1 hour. Pinch off egg-size lumps of dough and roll them into balls. Place them a fair distance apart on a buttered baking tray or trays. Cover and leave to rise in a warm place until doubled in size (about 2 hours). Preheat the oven to 375° F (190° C, gas mark 5). Beat the remaining egg and brush the tops of the buns with it. Sprinkle sesame seeds over and bake for 30 minutes or until the buns are nicely browned.

Freeze any buns not needed immediately, and use them later. Alternatively, slightly stale buns can be split and toasted.

Bagels

Bagels are a popular snack food, and in many countries of the Middle East they can be bought from street vendors. They are at their best warm and fresh, straight from the oven, accompanied by hot coffee.

Makes about 20 bagels

1 lb (450 g) plain flour
1 teaspoon salt
1 oz (12.5 g) fresh yeast, *or*
1 teaspoon dried yeast
4 fl oz (100 ml) warm water

¼ teaspoon sugar
4 oz (100 g) margarine, melted
1 egg, beaten
sesame seeds for topping

Sift together the flour and salt. Dissolve the yeast and sugar in the water and set aside in a warm place until the mixture starts to bubble. Add the yeast mixture to the flour and salt and stir in the margarine. Mix well to form a firm but not stiff dough – you may need to add a little more water. Cover with a damp towel and set aside in a warm place for 1½ hours. Preheat the oven to 375° F (190° C, gas mark 5). Pinch off small pieces of dough weighing about 2 oz (50 g) and roll them into pencil-thick strips about 8 in (20.5 cm) long. Form them into circles and brush each with beaten egg. Sprinkle them with sesame seeds. Transfer the bagels to un-greased baking trays. Leave for 10 minutes to rise and then bake for 20 minutes or until nicely browned. •

For Jewish bagels put the unbaked bagels (before brushing with beaten eggs) one by one into a large pan of boiling water and remove them as they rise to the surface. Transfer them to lightly greased baking trays and leave them to rise for 10 minutes. Now brush the boiled bagels with beaten egg, sprinkle them with sesame seeds and bake in a preheated oven at 400° F (205° C, gas mark 6) for 15 minutes or until nicely browned.

Semits

Crisp rings of bread sprinkled with sesame seeds which are normally sold as a snack food. A common sound in the towns of Turkey is the shouts of '*Semit*' from bakers' boys, who carry the *semits* around threaded on long poles thrown over one shoulder.

Makes about 12 *semits*

1 lb (450 g) flour
1 teaspoon salt
4 oz (100 g) margarine, melted
2 fl oz (50 ml) milk

2 fl oz (50 ml) water
1 egg, beaten
sesame seeds for topping

Preheat the oven to 400° F (205° C, gas mark 6). Sift the flour and salt together and place in a large bowl. Make a well in the centre and pour in all the remaining ingredients except the sesame seeds. Beat the mixture into a firm dough, adding more water if needed. Pinch off small pieces of dough and roll them into 8 in (20.5 cm) lengths about ½ in (1 cm) in diameter. Form each into a circle, brush with a little milk and sprinkle with sesame seeds. Bake the *semits* for 30 minutes or until nicely browned.

Salted sesame biscuits

12 oz (350 g) flour
2 teaspoons salt
1 teaspoon baking powder
1 egg, beaten

2 oz (50 g) sesame seeds
2 tablespoons vegetable oil
4 fl oz (100 ml) water

Combine all the ingredients and mix into a smooth but firm dough. Add a little more water if needed. Preheat the oven to 375° F (190° C, gas mark 5). Roll out the dough to biscuit thickness and cut out rounds. Transfer them to an ungreased baking tray and bake for about 20 minutes or until the biscuits are browned and crisp.

GRAINS AND PULSES

The Middle East is the source of many of today's common species of wheat grain. Thousands of years ago the successful cultivation, trade and storage of wheat led to the development in the region of some of the earliest great civilizations. Today wheat products are still particularly important in the Middle East. Bread is the most common of them, but other wheat grain foods such as bulgar wheat and couscous are widely used. Couscous, the national dish of Morocco, Tunisia and Algeria, was introduced into Middle Eastern cuisine by the Berbers, who lived in parts of North Africa long before the Arab (Moslem) invasion of the eighth century.

In relatively more recent times the cultivation of rice spread from India to Persia and then to the rest of the Middle East, and rice is now an important grain product and an intrinsic ingredient of Middle Eastern cuisine. The Iranians are particular connoisseurs of rice and they grow many varieties. Perhaps the most interesting and certainly the most expensive is the *domsiah* or black tail rice, which has a tiny black fleck at the end of each grain.

Pulses and grains are both important protein sources and both were cultivated in early times. Pulses, particularly lentils, are mentioned in the records of Ancient Egypt and in the Old Testament. Many types of pulse are available today; they are a popular staple in the Middle East, along with bread, olive oil, olives and rice. The recipes given in this chapter are for substantial bean and lentil dishes. Further recipes which use pulses as ingredients are given in the chapters on salads, soups and *mezze*.

Bulgar wheat

Bulgar wheat, although relatively unknown in the West, is the staple food of some countries in the Middle East. It is prepared by parboiling wholewheat grains in the minimum amount of water. The wheat is then spread thickly on a cloth or tray, dried in the sun and finally cracked between stone rollers. Bulgar is served and used in the same ways as rice might be, and also as the base for a variety of cold salads. It has all the nutritional qualities of wholewheat grain, plus a distinctive taste, and it is easy to cook. Bulgar is now available in many health and wholefood stores. In most recipes cracked wheat may be substituted for traditional bulgar.

Recipes for bulgar and lentil pilar and bulgar and lentil cakes are given on p. 83, in the section on lentils and beans.

Plain bulgar wheat

Bulgar wheat is cooked by boiling or steaming after initial dry roasting or light sautéing in oil or butter. Fine grades are sometimes just soaked in hot water with no further cooking.

Recipe 1

8 oz (225 g) bulgar wheat
16 fl oz (450 ml) water
salt

Dry roast the bulgar wheat in a heavy saucepan over a medium heat for 2 to 3 minutes, stirring constantly. Remove from the heat, allow to cool for a couple of minutes, and then add the water. Bring to the boil, reduce the heat, cover and simmer for 25 to 30 minutes or until all the water is absorbed. Salt to taste towards the end of the cooking time.

Recipe 2

4 tablespoons vegetable oil   16 fl oz (450 ml) water or stock
1 clove garlic, crushed   salt, black pepper and cayenne
8 oz (225 g) bulgar wheat   to taste

Heat the oil in a heavy pan, add the garlic and lightly sauté. Add the bulgar wheat and gently fry, stirring, for 2 to 3 minutes. Pour in the stock or water and simmer over a very low heat for 30 to 45 minutes, or until all the water is absorbed. Towards the end of the cooking time season to taste with salt, pepper and cayenne.

Pine nuts make a really delicious addition to bulgar wheat. Fry 1 oz (25 g) pine nuts in the oil along with the garlic in recipe 2, and then proceed as before.

Bulgar wheat pilav

2 oz (50 g) butter or vegetable
    oil
1 medium onion, diced
12 oz (350 g) bulgar wheat

1 pt (575 ml) stock or water
salt and black pepper to taste
8 fl oz (225 ml) yoghurt

Melt the butter in a heavy frying pan and sauté the onion until it is just starting to brown. Add the wheat and stir well so that each grain is coated in the butter or oil. Leave to cook over a very low heat for 10 minutes and then stir in the water or stock. Season to taste with salt and black pepper, and leave to simmer gently for 15 minutes or until all the liquid is absorbed. Remove from the heat, leave to stand for 5 minutes, fluff with a fork and serve with a bowl of yoghurt. The pilav can be served on its own with a salad or as an accompaniment to a main dish.

Baked bulgar wheat pilav

Serves 6 to 8

2 pts (1.1 l) stock
1 lb (450 g) bulgar wheat
1 teaspoon salt
½ teaspoon black pepper
4 oz (100 g) butter

1 medium onion, diced
4 oz (100 g) breadcrumbs
2 tablespoons chopped fresh
    parsley

Preheat the oven to 350°F (175°C, gas mark 4). Bring the stock to the boil in a large pan. Add the bulgar wheat and seasoning and simmer covered for 30 minutes. Melt half the butter in a frying pan, add the onion and fry golden brown. Stir this into the cooked bulgar and transfer the mixture to an ovenproof casserole. Bake uncovered for 20 minutes. Combine the parsley and breadcrumbs and sprinkle the mixture over the baked wheat. Dot the surface with the remaining butter and bake for a further 10 minutes.

Variation
Add mushrooms and green peppers, and replace the breadcrumbs with cheese.

Bulgar wheat and noodle pilav

2 oz (50 g) butter or oil
4 oz (100 g) fine egg noodles
8 oz (225 g) bulgar wheat

16 fl oz (450 ml) stock or water
1 teaspoon dried basil
salt and black pepper to taste

Melt the butter in a heavy saucepan or frying pan and add the noodles. Sauté over a low heat, stirring until the noodles are lightly browned. Add the bulgar wheat and cook and stir another minute or two. Pour in the stock, add the basil, stir well and season to taste with salt and black pepper. Bring to the boil, reduce heat and gently simmer for 20 minutes or until all the liquid is absorbed. If the liquid dries up before the mixture tastes properly cooked, add more as necessary.

Syrian bulgar salad

Serves 6 to 8

12 oz (350 g) fine bulgar wheat
1 large onion, finely diced
2 fl oz (50 ml) olive oil or other vegetable oil
4 oz (100 g) tomato paste
2 oz (50 g) pine nuts or chopped walnuts
1 tablespoon dried oregano

2 tablespoons chopped fresh parsley
1 teaspoon ground coriander
1 teaspoon ground cumin
½ teaspoon ground allspice
salt, black pepper and cayenne to taste

Cover the bulgar wheat in cold water and leave to soak for 30 minutes. Drain well. Sauté the onion in a little of the oil until just soft and transparent. Combine the onion and remaining ingredients with the bulgar wheat and mix well together. Put in the refrigerator for 2 to 3 hours or longer to allow the flavours to blend, and then serve.

Bulgar wheat and spinach

2 oz (50 g) butter or vegetable oil
2 cloves garlic, crushed
1 large onion, finely sliced
8 oz (225 g) bulgar wheat

16 fl oz (450 ml) stock or water
12 oz (350 g) spinach, washed and chopped
salt and black pepper to taste

Melt the butter in a heavy saucepan and sauté the garlic and onion until golden. Set the pan and contents aside. Combine the water or stock and bulgar wheat in another pan and bring to the boil. Reduce heat and simmer for 15 minutes. Add the bulgar wheat, spinach, salt and black pepper to the sautéed onions and garlic, and mix well. Simmer very gently, stirring occasionally, for another 15 minutes. Adjust seasoning and serve.

Couscous

This is probably the most common and most widely known North African Arab dish. Couscous is a grain product made from semolina, and it is also the name of the famous dish of which couscous is the main ingredient. Until recent times couscous grain was always made by hand, a tricky job requiring skill and experience, but nowadays, fortunately, it is available prepared and only needs cooking. The couscous is steamed over a rich sauce or stew and then served in a mountainous heap with the sauce poured over. It is never cooked in the sauce. A special pot called a *couscousier* is traditionally used for cooking the sauce and simultaneously steaming the couscous, but a saucepan with a snug-fitting colander on top will do just as well.

Orthodox couscous is made with mutton or chicken, but a vegetable sauce can be just as successful – below is a suggested recipe. As long as the method and seasoning are followed precisely the combination of vegetables may be altered according to season.

Vegetable couscous

Serves 6 to 8

2 oz (50 g) butter or vegetable oil
3 cloves garlic, crushed
2 medium onions, quartered
6 small courgettes, cut in 1 in (2.5 cm) pieces
2 medium green peppers, seeded, cored and cut in thick strips
2 large potatoes, scrubbed or peeled, and coarsely chopped

2 pt (1.1 l) water
1 lb (450 g) couscous
8 oz (225 g) chick peas, cooked and drained
1 lb (450 g) fresh tomatoes, quartered, *or*
1 lb (450 g) tinned tomatoes
4 oz (100 g) sultanas, apricots or raisins, soaked and drained
1½ teaspoons ground coriander
1½ teaspoons ground cumin

4 medium carrots, peeled, cut
  in half crosswise, then sliced
  in half lengthwise
2 small turnips, cut in half, then
  sliced lengthwise

2 teaspoons turmeric
½ teaspoon cayenne
2 small chilli peppers, seeded
  and chopped
salt and black pepper to taste

In a heavy saucepan or in the bottom of a *couscousier* melt the butter, add the next seven ingredients and sauté, stirring, over a moderate heat for 10 minutes. Add half the water and bring to the boil. Reduce the heat and simmer for 30 minutes. Meanwhile place the couscous in a large bowl and gently stir in 1 pt (575 ml) cold water. Drain immediately and allow the wet grains to stand for 10 to 15 minutes. As they swell up rake them with your fingers to prevent lumps forming. Turn the grains into the top of a *couscousier* or into a colander and place it over the cooking vegetables. Leave to steam gently for 30 minutes. Remove the top of the *couscousier* or the colander and add to the vegetables the remaining ingredients. Bring the vegetables to the boil and then reduce the heat and simmer for 15 minutes. Stir the couscous grains to break up any lumps that have formed and put the couscous back over the cooking vegetables. Cook and steam for a final 20 minutes. Pile the grains on a large serving dish. Drain off some of the liquid from the vegetables into a separate bowl. Pour the vegetables over the couscous and serve with the cooking liquid and hot pepper sauce or *harissa* in separate bowls.

Couscous with sweet Moroccan sauce

4 oz (100 g) butter
2 medium onions, diced small
2 tablespoons ground cinnamon
½ teaspoon saffron or turmeric
1 teaspoon ground ginger
½ teaspoon black pepper

1 teaspoon salt
12 fl oz (350 ml) water
4 oz (100 g) sugar
8 oz (225 g) raisins, soaked
  overnight and drained
1 lb (450 g) couscous

Melt the butter in a heavy pan, add the onion, spices and seasoning and sauté until the onion is soft and golden. Pour in the water, sugar and raisins, bring to the boil, reduce heat, cover and cook for 25 to 30 minutes. The sauce should be quite thick by this time, but if it isn't remove the lid and reduce the liquid a little over a moderate heat. Meanwhile steam the couscous over a pan of boiling water for 30 to 35 minutes. If by this time it is not cooked, sprinkle 5 fl oz (150 ml) of water over it and stir with a wooden spoon. Continue steaming until cooked. Pile the cooked grains on a serving dish, make a hollow in the top, fill with the sweet sauce and serve.

Millet

Millet is eaten in some of the Middle Eastern countries, although in the West its popularity has declined. This is a pity since millet is easy to prepare and has an enjoyable nutty flavour.

Persian millet pilav

8 oz (225 g) millet, washed and drained
3 tablespoons vegetable oil
1 clove garlic, crushed
salt to taste
8 fl oz (225 ml) water
1 medium onion, diced
2 oz (50 g) nuts (e.g. pistachio, almonds, pine nuts or walnuts)

2 medium tomatoes, sliced, for garnishing
chopped parsley or mint for garnishing
8 fl oz (225 ml) yoghurt

Heat half the oil in a heavy pan and add the millet. Stir fry over a moderate heat until the millet starts to colour. Add the garlic, salt and water, bring to the boil, reduce heat and simmer covered until all the water is absorbed – about 15 minutes. In a frying pan sauté the onion golden in the remaining oil. Gently brown the nuts under a moderate grill. Stir the nuts and onions into the cooked millet. Serve garnished with parsley or mint and tomatoes and accompanied by a bowl of yoghurt.

Rice

Rice is not an indigenous crop to the Middle East but was probably introduced from the Far East thousands of years ago. It grows well in some areas but in others is more scarce, and it is not considered a poor man's food. Rice is generally served either plain cooked with a sauce to pour over, or as a pilav (*polo* in Iran) in which the rice is cooked with a combination of other ingredients. Pilavs can be very simple, containing only one or two vegetables, or rich and exotic with an abundance of exciting ingredients. The cooked pilav rice should be just moist with grains that remain separate.

For plain cooked rice dishes 1 lb (450 g) rice is enough for 4 to 6 people, while in pilav dishes 8 oz (225 g) rice is about right for 4 people. For all the recipes use good-quality long grain rice which has been thoroughly washed and drained.

Plain cooked rice

Two methods are given. In the first, most widely used recipe, the rice is cooked in water with salt and some butter or margarine. The second is the method used in Iran, where the cooking of rice has been developed to a fine art and where rice or a rice dish accompanies most meals.

General method

Quantities are given in volumes, since it is the volume of water relative to the volume of rice that is important, rather than weight. One cup is assumed to equal 8 fl oz (225 ml) water or 8 oz (225 g) rice.

1½ cups long grain rice
2 cups water
2 tablespoons butter or
  margarine
1 teaspoon salt

Put the rice in a colander and wash under running water until the water runs clear. Now leave the rice to drain completely. Bring the water, butter and salt to the boil in a heavy pan. Stir in the rice and return to the boil. Reduce the heat, cover the pan with a tight-fitting lid, and simmer for 20 minutes. The rice should now be tender, the grains separate and all the water absorbed. Leave the pan covered, remove it from the heat and leave it to stand for 10 minutes. The rice is now ready to serve.

If you do not have a pan with a tight-fitting lid, place a clean tea towel between the pan and lid. Be careful not to let it dangle in the gas flames or on the hot plate.

For particularly flavoursome rice substitute vegetable or other stock for the water, or use one of the variations on the general method given below.

Minted rice

Cook the rice as described in the general method, but sprinkle 2 tablespoons of crushed dried mint over it when it is removed from the heat before standing for 10 minutes. Serve with salads, yoghurt, cheese and bread.

Yellow rice

Cook the rice as described in the general method, but add to the pot at the beginning of the cooking time ½ teaspoon of powdered saffron or turmeric. Serve with vegetables.

Rice with orange juice

Cook the rice by the general method. When it is cooked stir in 8 fl oz (225 ml) fresh orange juice and a pinch of allspice. Simmer for 3 minutes. Serve with fruit salad or vegetables.

Iranian method (chelo rice)

1½ cups basmati or long grain rice, soaked in water for 4 to 6 hours or overnight	4 pt (2 l) water
	3 oz (75 g) butter or margarine, melted
1 tablespoon salt	2 tablespoons water

Drain the rice well and wash it under running cold water until the water runs clear. Drain again. Bring the salt and water to the boil and gradually stir in the rice. Return to the boil and boil rapidly for 8 minutes or until the rice is not quite tender. At this stage the centre of a rice grain should not be hard, but the rice should still be a little chewy. Strain the rice, rinse with a little warm water and leave to drain thoroughly. Put 1 tablespoon of the butter and the 2 tablespoons of water in the bottom of a heavy pan. Mound the rice into the pan, forming a rough cone shape. Make a hole down the centre of the cone with the handle of a wooden spoon and pour down the hole the remaining melted butter. Wrap the lid of the saucepan in a clean tea towel, keeping the ends well tucked in, and put the lid on. The towel absorbs any rising steam and the rice grains stay fluffy and separate. Put the pan on a low heat and simmer for 20 to 25 minutes.

The rice at the bottom of the pan forms a golden crust which can be scraped off and served as a delicacy on its own or used to garnish the rice.

Rice cooked in this fashion, known as *chelo* rice, is served with one of a variety of sauces called *khoreshe*, for which recipes follow.

Sauces (khoreshe) for rice

Khoreshe are thick sauces or stews traditionally served with *chelo* rice (although there is no reason why they should not accompany plain cooked rice if you wish). In Iran a *khoreshe* and rice will be served once, maybe twice, a day and it is important for the Iranian cook to be skilled in their preparation. The *khoreshe* can be made from a wide variety of ingredients combined in an endless number of ways. Normally they contain meat or poultry, but below are four which contain only vegetables, fruits and nuts.

Courgette khoreshe

1 lb (450 g) cooked chelo rice
  or plain cooked rice
2 oz (50 g) butter or margarine
2 medium courgettes, cut in ¼
  in (6 mm) slices
2 medium onions, sliced
2 medium red or green peppers,
  seeded, cored and cut in
  strips
8 oz (225 g) tomatoes, skinned
  and chopped

juice of 1 lemon
1 teaspoon ground cinnamon
½ teaspoon paprika
¼ teaspoon ground nutmeg
¼ teaspoon turmeric
salt and black pepper to taste
1 clove garlic
1 tablespoon fresh mint, *or*
1 teaspoon dried mint

Melt the butter in a heavy pot. Add the courgettes and three-quarters of the onions and sauté over a moderate heat until softened but not browned. Put in the peppers, tomatoes, lemon juice and seasonings and stir well. Bring the mixture to the boil, reduce heat, cover and simmer, stirring occasionally, for 20 to 30 minutes. Add a little water if it gets dry. Meanwhile sauté the reserved onion with the garlic and mint in a little oil or butter until golden. Put the courgette *khoreshe* in a bowl, garnish with the onion and mint mixture, and serve with the cooked rice.

Vegetable and lemon khoreshe

1 lb (450 g) cooked *chelo* rice or
  plain cooked rice
2 oz (50 g) butter or margarine
1 medium onion, thinly sliced
2 medium carrots, cut in 1 in
  (2.5 cm) matchsticks
4 oz (100 g) green beans, fresh
  or frozen, cut in 1 in (2.5 cm)
  lengths

2 oz (50 g) nuts (almonds, pine
  nuts, pistachios, walnuts
  etc.), chopped
juice of 1 lemon
peel of 1 lemon, grated
1 teaspoon ground cinnamon
½ teaspoon ground nutmeg
salt and black pepper to taste

Melt the butter in a heavy pan and sauté the onions and carrots over a moderate heat. Cook, stirring occasionally, for 5 minutes. Add all the remaining ingredients except the rice, mix well, bring to the boil, reduce heat, cover and simmer for 30 minutes, stirring occasionally. Serve in a separate bowl from the cooked rice.

Almond and pine nut khoreshe

The pine nuts required for this recipe are expensive, so by all means experiment with another type of nut. Cook the rice to be served with this sauce with a little turmeric to give some colour to the dish.

1 lb (450 g) cooked *chelo* rice or
    plain cooked rice
4 oz (100 g) ground almonds
1 pt (575 ml) stock or water
1 clove garlic, crushed
2 tablespoons chopped fresh
    parsley

1 teaspoon sugar
juice of 1 lemon
salt and black pepper to taste
2 oz (50 g) pine nuts, lightly
    toasted

Put the ground almonds and stock or water in a heavy pot and bring to the boil. Add the garlic, parsley, sugar, lemon juice, seasoning and half the pine nuts. Mix well and simmer gently, uncovered, for 20 to 30 minutes or until the sauce is quite thick. Garnish with the reserved nuts, and serve the sauce and rice in separate bowls.

Aubergine and lentil khoreshe

1 lb (450 g) cooked *chelo* rice or
    plain cooked rice
2 oz (50 g) butter or margarine
3 to 4 medium aubergines,
    sliced
1 medium onion, finely sliced
3 oz (75 g) whole brown or
    green lentils, soaked for 4
    hours, then drained

juice of 1 lemon
2 tablespoons tomato paste
½ teaspoon ground cinnamon
½ teaspoon paprika
pinch ground nutmeg
pinch turmeric
salt and black pepper to taste

Salt the aubergine slices and place them in a colander under a weight for 30 minutes. Meanwhile melt half the butter in a heavy pot and sauté the onion golden, then add the lentils and stir fry for 2 to 3 minutes. Add all the remaining ingredients except the rice, aubergines and reserved butter and mix well. Pour in cold water to cover the lentils and bring to the boil. Reduce heat, cover and leave to simmer for 1 hour or until the lentils are tender.

Rinse the aubergines and fry them brown on both sides in the remaining butter. Put them in the pot with the lentils and cook over a moderate heat for a further 15 minutes or until the aubergines are definitely tender. Serve the *khoreshe* and rice in separate bowls.

Pilav rice dishes

Basic pilav rice

Serve with main dishes or on its own with a sauce (see p. 114).

2 oz (50 g) butter or margarine
1 medium onion, finely sliced
1 cup long grain rice, washed
   thoroughly and drained
1 clove garlic

1½ cups water or stock
salt to taste
fresh parsley or paprika for
   garnish

Melt the butter in a heavy pan and sauté the onion until it is just softened. Add the rice and garlic and sauté, stirring, for 2 to 3 minutes. Pour in the water or stock and season to taste with salt. Bring to the boil, reduce heat, cover with a tight-fitting lid and simmer for 20 minutes. Leave covered during this time. Remove the pan from the heat and leave to stand for 10 minutes. Toss the rice with a fork and serve.

Pilav with noodles

This is another basic dish to accompany main dishes or to be served on its own with a sauce (see p. 114).

2 oz (50 g) butter or margarine
1 medium onion, finely
   chopped
2 oz (50 g) raisins, soaked and
   drained (optional)
4 oz (100 g) fine egg noodles
   (Chinese or vermicelli types)

1 cup long grain rice, washed
   thoroughly and drained
2 cups water or stock
salt to taste

Melt the butter in a heavy pan and sauté the onion until soft and golden. Add the raisins, if used and sauté for 2 to 3 minutes. Stir in the noodles and fry, stirring, until they lightly colour. Add the rice and continue stirring and cooking over a low heat until all the grains are coated in oil. Pour in the water, season to taste with salt and bring to the boil. Reduce the heat, cover with a tight-fitting lid and simmer for 20 minutes. Leave covered during this time. Remove from the heat and leave to stand for 10 minutes. Fluff up the pilav with a fork and serve.

Sultan's pilav

This Turkish dish is traditionally made with pistachio nuts, but you can equally well substitute pine nuts or even chopped walnuts or cashews.

4 oz (100 g) butter or margarine
1 lb (450 g) long grain rice, washed thoroughly and drained
1¼ pt (725 ml) stock or water
2 oz (50 g) sultanas, soaked for 1 hour and drained

pinch saffron or turmeric
½ teaspoon allspice
2 oz (50 g) pistachios or other nuts
salt and black pepper to taste

Melt the butter in a heavy saucepan. Add the rice and sauté, stirring, until each grain is coated in butter. Add the remaining ingredients, except for 1 tablespoon of the nuts, and bring the mixture to the boil. Reduce the heat, cover the pan with a tight-fitting lid and simmer for 20 minutes. Remove the pan from the heat and allow to stand for 10 minutes. Meanwhile lightly toast and then finely chop the reserved nuts. Tip the pilav on to a serving dish and garnish with the chopped, toasted nuts.

Savoury pilav

This is not a fixed recipe, and if you wish you may substitute other vegetables than those suggested.

Serves 6

4 oz (100 g) butter or margarine
2 medium onions, diced
2 cloves garlic, crushed
½ teaspoon ground cloves
1 teaspoon ground cinnamon
½ teaspoon ground ginger
12 oz (350 g) long grain rice, washed thoroughly and drained
pinch saffron or turmeric
1 tablespoon fresh parsley, *or* 1 teaspoon dried parsley

1¼ pt (725 ml) water
juice of 1 lemon
2 medium tomatoes, quartered
3 medium carrots, peeled and finely sliced
6 oz (175 g) green peas, fresh or frozen
2 oz (50 g) sultanas, soaked for 1 hour and drained
salt and black pepper to taste
2 oz (50 g) pine nuts or other nuts for garnishing

Melt the butter in a large, heavy saucepan and sauté the onion and garlic until golden. Add the cloves, cinnamon, ginger, turmeric or saffron and rice, and stir fry over a low heat for 4 to 5 minutes. Add the water, parsley, lemon juice, tomatoes, carrots, peas and sultanas and mix well. Season to taste with salt and black pepper. Bring to the boil, reduce heat, cover the pan with a tight-fitting lid and cook over a low heat for 20 minutes. Remove the pan from the heat and allow to stand for 5 to 10 minutes. Meanwhile lightly toast the nuts. Pile the pilav on a serving plate and garnish with the toasted nuts.

Fruit and nut pilav

This pilav, although sweet, can be served as a main course. It is very pleasant served on a summer evening with a chilled side salad. On colder days the water in the recipe can be replaced with milk to make a very nourishing meal.

4 oz (100 g) butter or margarine
4 oz (100 g) dried apricots, soaked overnight, drained and chopped
2 oz (50 g) sultanas, soaked for 1 hour and drained
4 oz (100 g) dates, chopped
2 oz (50 g) pine nuts or blanched almonds, lightly roasted

1 tablespoon sugar or honey
8 oz (225 g) long grain rice, thoroughly washed and drained
16 fl oz (450 ml) water, *or*
12 fl oz (350 ml) water plus 4 fl oz (100 ml) orange juice

Melt the butter in a heavy pan and add the apricots, sultanas and dates. Cook, stirring occasionally, for 5 minutes. Add the nuts, honey and rice, stir and cook for another 5 minutes. Add the water or water and orange juice mixture and bring to the boil. Reduce the heat, cover the pot with a tight-fitting lid, and simmer for 20 minutes. Remove from the heat, allow to stand for 5 minutes, transfer to a serving dish and serve.

Iranian vegetable polo

This exotic blend of fruit and vegetables is the Iranian, and some say original, version of pilav rice. It is traditionally cooked on the top of the stove, but can equally well be baked in the oven. Instructions for both methods are given.

Serves 6 to 8

1 lb (450 g) basmati or long
  grain rice, thoroughly
  washed and drained
4 tablespoons butter or
  vegetable oil
2 medium onions, thinly sliced
1 clove garlic, crushed
1 medium green pepper,
  seeded, cored and sliced
2 medium carrots, thinly sliced
4 oz (100 g) garden peas, fresh
  or frozen
2 oz (50 g) dried apricots,
  soaked overnight, drained
  and chopped

2 oz (50 g) raisins, soaked 1
  hour and drained
2 oz (50 g) blanched almonds or
  other nuts
2 tablespoons grated orange
  peel
1 teaspoon ground cinnamon
½ teaspoon ground nutmeg
salt and black pepper to taste
4 fl oz (100 ml) water or stock

Parboil the rice as for *chelo* rice (see p. 76). Stop at the stage when
the rice is just parboiled and described as chewy. Melt half the butter
in a heavy frying pan and add the onions, pepper, garlic and carrots.
Cook them, stirring occasionally, for 5 minutes or until the vegetables are just softened. Add the peas and continue cooking another
3 to 4 minutes. Season to taste with salt and black pepper. In another
pan melt half the remaining butter and cook in it the apricots,
raisins, almonds, cinnamon and nutmeg for 5 minutes, stirring occasionally. Coat the bottom of a big, heavy pan (the pan can be
replaced by a casserole dish and the *polo* is then baked in a preheated
oven at 350° F (175° C, gas mark 4) for 30 minutes) with the
remaining butter and spread half of the parboiled rice over this.
Cover with the onions and vegetable mixture. Spread half the remaining rice over this, and on top spread the fruit and nut mixture.
Top with the remaining rice, pour in the water or stock and cover
the pan with a tight-fitting lid or use a lid wrapped in a clean tea
towel with the ends tucked in. Simmer over a low heat for 20 to 25
minutes. The rice should by then be fluffy. Tip the *polo* on to a large
serving dish, scrape the bottom of the pan, and use the crust for
garnish.

Spinach pilav

In this Turkish recipe the rice is cooked in the water released by the
spinach during cooking. It is a simple but effective method which
gives a very tasty pilav-style dish.

2 oz (50 g) margarine or butter
1 large onion, finely sliced
1½ lb (675 g) spinach, washed
and well chopped

4 oz (100 g) rice
4 fl oz (100 g) thinned tomato
paste
salt and pepper to taste

Melt the butter in a heavy pot and sauté the onion lightly. Layer the spinach on top and press down, then pour in the rice and slightly thinned tomato paste, and season to taste with salt and black pepper. Cover the pot with a tight-fitting lid and gently simmer for 20 minutes or until the rice is tender. Do not remove the lid more than necessary, and do not stir. Transfer to a warm dish and serve.

Lentil and bean dishes

Lentil pilav

4 oz (100 g) butter
2 medium onions, diced
2 cloves garlic, crushed
2 tablespoons chopped fresh
parsley
1½ teaspoons ground coriander

1½ teaspoons ground cumin
salt and black pepper to taste
8 oz (225 g) cooked rice,
drained
1 lb (450 g) cooked lentils,
drained

Melt the butter in a heavy frying pan and add the onions, garlic, parsley, cumin and coriander. Sauté, stirring, until the onions are soft and golden. Stir in the cooked rice and lentils, season to taste and gently heat through. Serve with a green salad and a bowl of olives.

Syrian lentils with noodles

2 tablespoons vegetable oil	salt and black pepper to taste
1 large onion, diced	8 oz (225 g) noodles or
2 cloves garlic, crushed	spaghetti, cooked and drained
½ teaspoon ground cumin	2 oz (50 g) melted butter
½ teaspoon ground coriander	
16 oz (450 g) cooked lentils, drained	

Put the oil in a heavy saucepan and add the onion and garlic. Sauté until golden. Add the cumin and coriander and toss in the lentils. Stir well and heat through. Season to taste with salt and black pepper. Add the freshly cooked noodles and gently mix. Transfer to a warmed serving dish and pour the melted butter over the top.

Variation
Layer the onion mixture, lentils and spaghetti in a baking dish and pour over tomato sauce (see p. 114). Sprinkle 4 oz (100 g) grated cheese over the top and bake in a preheated oven at 375° F (190° C, gas mark 5) for 30 minutes.

Megadarra

This dish of lentils and rice is sometimes known as Esau's dish, since it was said to be the favourite dish of the poor.

4 tablespoons butter or vegetable oil	1 teaspoon ground cumin
8 oz (225 g) lentils, soaked and drained	1 teaspoon ground allspice
	salt and black pepper to taste
1¼ pt (725 ml) water	1 clove garlic, crushed
8 oz (225 g) rice, washed and drained	2 medium onions, finely sliced
	8 fl oz (225 ml) yoghurt

Heat half the butter or vegetable oil in a heavy pan, add the lentils and stir fry for 2 to 3 minutes. Add the water, bring to the boil, reduce the heat and simmer for 15 minutes. Add the rice, cumin, allspice, and salt and pepper to taste. Return to the boil and mix well. Reduce the heat and simmer until the lentils and rice are tender and all the water is absorbed (15 to 20 minutes). Meanwhile sauté the garlic and onion dark golden in the remaining butter or oil. Tip the lentils and rice into a serving bowl, mix in three-quarters of the onions, pour the yoghurt over and garnish the top with the remaining onions.

Courgettes stuffed with lentils

2 large courgettes
2 tablespoons vegetable oil
1 medium onion, diced
1 clove garlic, crushed
1 teaspoon ground cinnamon
¼ teaspoon ground nutmeg

12 oz (350 g) cooked lentils, drained
salt and black pepper to taste
2 tablespoons chopped walnuts or pine nuts

Preheat the oven to 375° F (190° C, gas mark 5). Halve the courgettes lengthwise and scoop out the pulp, leaving a shell ½ to ¾ in (1.3 to 1.8 cm) thick. Chop the pulp and reserve. Heat the oil in a heavy frying pan and sauté the onion and garlic until golden. Add the reserved pulp, cinnamon and nutmeg and gently sauté for a further 10 minutes. Combine this mixture with the cooked lentils and season to taste with salt and black pepper. Stuff the courgette shells with the mixture and place them in a greased baking dish. Sprinkle the nuts over the top and cover the dish with a lid or aluminium foil. Bake for 25 to 30 minutes or until the courgettes are tender.

Apples stuffed with lentils

4 medium to large cooking apples, cored
4 fl oz (100 ml) water
4 oz (100 g) cooked lentils, drained
4 oz (100 g) cooked rice, drained
1 medium onion, diced

2 tablespoons butter
4 oz (100 g) sultanas, soaked and drained
2 teaspoons sugar
½ teaspoon ground cumin
½ teaspoon turmeric
½ teaspoon salt
¼ teaspoon black pepper

Cut the tops off the apples and scoop out the pulp, leaving shells about ¼ in (6 mm) thick. Mix the pulp with the water and cook, covered, until tender. Then remove the lid and simmer off the moisture until the pulp is quite firm. Meanwhile sauté the onions golden in the butter. Combine half the pulp, the onions, half the sultanas and all the remaining ingredients except the sugar. Mix well and stuff the apples with the mixture. Preheat the oven to 300° F (145° C, gas mark 2). Combine the remaining pulp and sultanas with the sugar and spread the mixture on the base of a lightly buttered baking dish. Pack in the stuffed apples and bake for 45 minutes.

Lentil and spinach pilav

4 oz (100 g) butter
3 cloves garlic, crushed
12 oz (350 g) spinach, washed and chopped
12 oz (350 g) cooked lentils, drained

1 tablespoon chopped fresh parsley
salt and black pepper to taste

Melt half the butter in a heavy pan and lightly sauté the garlic. Add the spinach and cook over a low heat until it has wilted. Stir in the remaining ingredients and sauté a further 5 minutes. Adjust seasoning and serve.

Chick peas with aubergines

2 medium aubergines cut into 2 in (5 cm) square cubes
2 medium onions, sliced
4 fl oz (100 ml) olive oil or other vegetable oil
1 lb (450 g) cooked chick peas, drained

8 oz (225 g) tinned tomatoes
1 tablespoon tomato paste
2 oz (50 g) pine nuts (optional)
1 teaspoon dried mint
salt and black pepper to taste

Generously salt the aubergine cubes and put in a colander to drain for 30 minutes. Now wash them under running water to remove excess salt, and pat dry on paper towels. Put the aubergines, onion and olive oil in a heavy frying pan and fry until the onion and aubergine are lightly browned. Add the remaining ingredients and cook over a low heat, uncovered, for 30 minutes. Serve hot as a main dish, with brown rice and a green salad, or cold as hors d'oeuvres.

Ful medames

This bean dish is almost the national food of Egypt and it can be bought there in thousands of small cafés and restaurants. The dish is traditionally served with tahini, lemon juice and pita bread, which is used as an eating scoop.

Serves 6

1 lb (450 g) *ful* beans, soaked
  overnight and drained
2½ pt (1.4 l) water
6 eggs
4 cloves garlic, crushed
3 tablespoons olive oil
1 tablespoon ground cumin
salt to taste

1 teaspoon paprika
1 teaspoon turmeric
tahini
2 tablespoons chopped fresh
  parsley
2 lemons, quartered
olive oil

Put the beans in a heavy saucepan with the water, unbroken eggs, garlic, olive oil and cumin. Bring to the boil, cover, reduce the heat and simmer on a very low heat for 6 hours or more. Towards the end of the cooking time season to taste with salt. Remove the eggs and shell them. Serve the beans sprinkled with paprika, accompanied by the eggs sprinkled with turmeric, and a bowl of tahini garnished with parsley and quartered lemons. Each person should crumble an egg over his or her beans, then squeeze on lemon juice and add olive oil as desired.

Egyptian bean salad

This is a salad made with *ful medames*, the brown beans so popular in Egypt.

1 lb (450 g) *ful medames* beans,
  soaked overnight and drained
juice of 1 lemon
2 fl oz (50 ml) olive oil

1 tablespoon finely chopped
  fresh parsley
2 cloves garlic, crushed
salt and black pepper to taste

Cover the beans in cold water, bring to the boil and reduce the heat. Simmer for 90 minutes or until very tender. Allow to cool, then drain. Mix the remaining ingredients and pour the mixture over the beans. Toss, then adjust the seasoning, olive oil and lemon juice until the salad is to your taste.

Black eye beans with spinach

8 oz (225 g) black eye beans,
  soaked overnight
2 tablespoons vegetable oil
1 medium onion, diced
1 lb (450 g) spinach, washed
  and chopped

4 oz (100 g) bulgar wheat
  (optional)
salt to taste
pinch of ground cloves

Drain the beans, cover them with fresh water and cook until soft. Drain, and reserve the liquid. Heat the oil in a heavy pan and lightly brown the onions, add the drained beans, 4 fl oz (110 ml) of the reserved liquid, spinach and bulgar wheat. Mix well, cover, and gently simmer until the spinach is wilted. Season to taste with salt and add the ground cloves. Stir, and simmer a few minutes more. Serve hot with olives and bread.

Red beans in oil

8 oz (225 g) red kidney beans, soaked overnight and drained
2 tablespoons olive oil or other vegetable oil
4 cloves garlic, crushed
1 medium onion, diced
salt and pepper to taste
2 medium tomatoes, quartered
fresh parsley, chopped, for garnishing

Cover the beans in cold water, bring to the boil, reduce the heat and simmer, covered, until the beans are tender but not disintegrating (about 1 hour). Strain, and reserve the cooking liquid. Heat the oil in a heavy pan and sauté the garlic and onion until golden, then add the tomatoes and sauté a further few minutes. Stir the beans and add 10 fl oz (275 ml) of the reserved cooking liquid to the pan. Season to taste with salt and black pepper and simmer over a low heat for 10 to 15 minutes. Serve hot as a side dish or chilled as a starter or salad. In both cases garnish with parsley before serving.

Arabian apple bean pot

Serves 6

1 lb (450 g) lima or butter beans, soaked overnight and drained
2½ pt (1.5 l) water
2 tablespoons vegetable oil or butter
2 medium onions, sliced
2 medium cooking apples, cored and sliced
½ teaspoon turmeric
½ teaspoon ground allspice
½ teaspoon ground cinnamon
salt and black pepper to taste
8 fl oz (225 ml) yoghurt
2 oz (50 g) dried apricots, chopped

Put the beans and water in a heavy saucepan and bring to the boil. Cover, reduce the heat and simmer until the beans are tender – about 1½ hours. Heat the oil in a large, heavy frying pan and sauté the onions until golden. Add the apple, turmeric, allspice and cinnamon and cook, stirring, until the apple is softened. Drain the beans and reserve the cooking liquid. Add the beans to the frying pan with just enough cooking liquid to wet the contents of the pan. Season to taste with salt and black pepper and simmer for 10 minutes. Serve with a bowl of yoghurt and chopped apricots.

Moroccan bean pot

This unusual bean pot is very filling and nutritious. The recipe will make enough to feed 4 hungry people or 6 of moderate appetite.

1 lb (450 g) haricot beans,
  soaked overnight and drained
2 medium onions, one left
  whole, the other finely diced
4 cloves garlic
2 pt (1.1 l) water

4 fl oz (100 ml) vegetable oil
1 bunch finely chopped parsley
1 teaspoon turmeric
1 teaspoon ground cumin
salt and black pepper to taste
3 eggs

Put the beans, the whole onion, whole cloves of garlic and water in a heavy pot and bring to the boil, reduce the heat and simmer, covered, until the beans are tender – about 1 hour. Remove the onion and cloves of garlic (if you can find them) from the pot. Heat the oil in a heavy frying pan, add the diced onion and sauté golden. Stir in the parsley, turmeric and cumin, mix well and pour the contents of the frying pan into the bean pot. Season to taste with salt and black pepper and simmer for 15 minutes. The beans should now be quite dry. If they are not, scoop or drain off some of the liquid and keep for later use in soups, etc. Now break into the hot beans the 3 eggs and mix well. Serve immediately.

Israeli breakfast beans

This is a popular breakfast dish in various parts of the Middle East. It has apparently been adopted as the Israeli army's favourite breakfast.

8 oz (225 g) haricot beans,
  soaked overnight and drained
4 large tomatoes, skinned and
  chopped
2 tablespoons butter or
  vegetable oil

1 large onion, finely sliced
3 cloves garlic, crushed
½ teaspoon dried basil
1 tablespoon chopped fresh
  parsley
salt and pepper to taste

Cover the beans in cold water, bring to the boil, reduce the heat and simmer, covered, until tender (about 1 hour). Heat the butter or oil in a heavy frying pan and add the onions. Sauté over a moderate heat until soft and transparent. Add the remaining ingredients and simmer over a low heat for 5 to 10 minutes. Strain the beans and discard the cooking liquid (unless you want to save it for soups, etc.). Salt the beans to taste, stir in the onion and tomato mixture and serve. Any leftovers can be used cold as part of a salad.

Bean plaki

A popular dish in which the beans are cooked with various vegetables or tomatoes, then chilled and dressed with oil and vinegar. It's also good hot, served with warm garlic bread. The ingredients vary slightly, according to whether you want to serve the dish hot or cold.

Serves 6

4 fl oz (100 ml) olive oil
2 cloves garlic, crushed
2 medium onions, finely sliced
1 medium carrot, diced
2 stalks celery with leaves,
  chopped
3 tablespoons chopped fresh
  parsley
1 bay leaf, crumbled
1 teaspoon oregano

6 medium tomatoes, peeled and
  chopped, *or*
1 lb (450 g) tinned tomatoes
1 lb (450 g) haricot beans,
  soaked overnight and drained
salt to taste
2 tablespoons vinegar
2 tablespoons olive oil or other
  vegetable oil
olives for garnish

Heat the 4 fl oz (100 ml) oil in a heavy saucepan, then add the garlic, onion, carrot and celery and sauté until soft but not browned. Stir in 2 tablespoons of the parsley, the bay leaf, oregano and tomatoes, stir well and simmer until thoroughly blended. Add the beans with enough water to cover them, and bring to the boil. Cover, reduce the heat and simmer for 1 to 1½ hours or until the beans are tender. Salt to taste, and serve hot.

Alternatively, to serve cold, chill the cooked dish, stir in 2 tablespoons each of vinegar and olive oil or other vegetable oil, and garnish with olives and the remaining tablespoon of chopped parsley.

Fasoulia

A haricot bean dish of Greek origin. Like the other bean dishes it can be served hot or cold depending on the weather, and whether it is being served as a starter, main or side dish. It's a very rich, garlicky dish and quite delicious.

8 oz (225 g) haricot beans,
  soaked overnight and drained
4 fl oz (100 ml) olive oil
1 small bulb of garlic cloves,
  peeled and crushed
1 bay leaf

1 teaspoon oregano
2 tablespoons tomato paste
salt and black pepper to taste
juice of 1 lemon
½ small onion, diced

Put the beans, oil, garlic, bay leaf and oregano in a heavy pot and simmer over a low heat for 15 minutes. Remove from the heat and carefully pour in enough boiling water to cover the beans by about 1 in (2.5 cm). Stir in the tomato paste and simmer the mixture, covered, over a very low heat for 2 to 2½ hours. Finally, season to taste with salt and black pepper, sprinkle in the lemon juice and serve garnished with diced raw onion.

Tablee

8 oz (225 g) barley
4 oz (100 g) cooked chick peas

1 pt (575 ml) yoghurt
salt to taste

Cover the barley with water and cook until tender. Drain and cool. Combine the barley, chick peas and yoghurt with salt to taste. Chill and serve. Traditionally this dish is served as a snack on hot afternoons.

Bulgar and lentil pilav

8 oz (225 g) whole lentils,
  soaked and drained
2 pt (1.1 l) water
2 medium onions, diced
4 fl oz (100 ml) olive oil or
  other vegetable oil

8 oz (225 g) bulgar wheat
salt and black pepper to taste
8 fl oz (225 ml) yoghurt
1 teaspoon paprika

In a heavy pan combine the lentils and two-thirds of the water and bring to the boil. Reduce the heat and set to simmer for 20 minutes. Meanwhile fry the onions in the oil until golden brown. Drain the oil from the frying pan into the simmering lentils. Pour the remaining one-third of the water on to the onions in the frying pan and simmer over a low heat for 10 minutes. Add the bulgar wheat and the contents of the frying pan to the lentils and season to taste with salt and black pepper. Cover and simmer for 25 to 30 minutes or until all the eater is absorbed. Serve hot, topped with yoghurt and garnished with paprika.

Bulgar and lentil cakes

1 pt (575 ml) water
2 oz (50 g) lentils, washed, soaked and drained
4 oz (100 g) bulgar wheat
2 tablespoons butter
1 medium onion, diced
1 teaspoon ground cumin
1 teaspoon paprika

1 teaspoon ground coriander seeds
salt to taste

Garnish
1 small lettuce
hot pepper sauce
tahini

Put the lentils and water in a heavy pot, bring to the boil, reduce the heat, cover, and simmer until the lentils are soft (about 30 to 45 minutes). Now add the bulgar wheat, mix well and set aside from the heat for 1 hour. Fry the onions golden brown in the butter, and stir in the spices. Remove from the heat. In a mixing bowl combine the lentils and bulgar wheat with the onion and spices and season to taste with salt, stirring well together. Form the mixture by hand into small, round cakes and serve on a bed of lettuce with small bowls of hot pepper sauce and tahini.

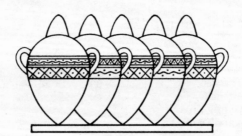

VEGETABLE DISHES

In Middle Eastern cooking vegetables are not always demoted to mere accompaniments to meat as they normally are in the West. In the markets a wonderful abundance of vegetables is available, and choosing them and haggling with the stallholder over the quality and price is an important part of the day's shopping. Incidentally this job is often done by men, not women. Generally the most popular vegetables are aubergines, celery, courgettes, cucumber, leeks, lettuce, onions, red and green peppers and tomatoes. Many of the recipes in this chapter are for substantial dishes, while the others can be served with soup or salads as a light meal.

Stuffed vegetables, or *mishshi* as they are called in Arabic, are a great speciality of Middle Eastern cuisine. Almost any vegetable available to the Middle Eastern cook is adapted to this way of cooking. Stuffings containing minced meat are common, but there are many rice-, nut- or vegetable-based fillings. The recipes in this chapter are for particular vegetables and fillings, but there is no reason why you should not use the filling in one recipe with the vegetable used in another, as long as the method given for preparing the particular vegetable for stuffing is followed (see p. 111).

A chapter on sauce recipes follows the vegetable recipes, and many of the sauces are suitable for serving with the vegetable dishes described in this chapter, particularly the stuffed vegetables.

Vegetable casseroles

Generally no two Middle Eastern vegetable casseroles or stews are the same, the contents depending on what is availabe and the imagination of the cook, but the following recipes give a general idea of the various vegetable combinations used in four Middle Eastern casseroles. As you will see, the cooking methods are very different, according to the country of origin.

Moroccan vegetable casserole

Serves 6 to 8

2 pt (1.1 l) water
2 teaspoons salt
4 to 6 cloves garlic, peeled
2 medium carrots, cubed
2 medium onions, diced
2 medium potatoes, peeled and cubed
1 small turnip, cubed

2 medium courgettes, thickly sliced
1 medium aubergine, cubed
4 tablespoons vegetable oil
1 to 2 hot chilli peppers, seeded and chopped
1 teaspoon ground cumin
2 tablespoons chopped parsley

Put the water and salt in a large pot and bring to the boil. Add the next seven ingredients, reserving half of the diced onion. Cover and return to the boil, reduce heat and simmer until all the vegetables are tender. Heat the oil in a heavy frying pan and sauté the reserved onion, chilli peppers, cumin and parsley until the onion is soft. Pour this mixture into the vegetable pot and simmer for a further 5 minutes.

Armenian vegetable casserole

Serves 6 to 8

4 tomatoes, thickly sliced
4 small carrots, sliced lengthwise into strips
4 medium onions, thickly sliced
2 medium courgettes, thickly sliced
2 medium aubergines, thickly sliced, salted, rinsed and drained
2 medium green peppers, seeded, cored and cut into strips

8 oz (225 g) okra (optional)
4 cloves garlic, finely chopped
4 tablespoons chopped fresh herbs, (mint, parsley, fennel, dill, etc.) *or*
4 teaspoons mixed dried herbs
4 fl oz (100 ml) olive oil or other vegetable oil
salt and pepper to taste

Oil a baking dish and layer the vegetables in it. Mix them up or keep them separate as you prefer but keep the tomatoes for the last layer. Between each layer sprinkle a little garlic, some herbs, some olive oil, and some salt and black pepper. Cover the dish and bake in a preheated oven at 350° F (175° C, gas mark 4) for 45 to 50 minutes or until all the vegetables are just tender but not mushy.

Turkish vegetable casserole

2 medium aubergines, thickly sliced, salted, rinsed and drained

2 medium green peppers, seeded cored and thickly sliced

2 medium courgettes, thickly sliced

8 oz (225 g) tomatoes, sliced

8 oz (225 g) French beans or other green beans, cut in 2 in (5 cm) pieces

4 cloves garlic, finely chopped

2 oz (50 g) butter

10 fl oz (275 ml) water or stock

salt and black pepper to taste

8 fl oz (225 ml) yoghurt

Melt the butter in a heavy frying pan and lightly brown the aubergines on both sides. Transfer to a baking dish. Put the other vegetables into the same frying pan and lightly sauté, stirring, pour them on top of the aubergines and add the garlic, water or stock and salt and black pepper to taste. Cover and bake in a preheated oven at 350° F (175° C, gas mark 4) for 1 hour or longer. Serve with a separate bowl of yoghurt.

Iranian green vegetable casserole

1 bunch spring onions or scallions, finely chopped

2 leeks, washed and chopped

8 oz (225 g) spinach, washed and chopped

½ lettuce, washed and chopped

1 bunch parsley, chopped

8 eggs, beaten

2 oz (50 g) walnuts, chopped

salt and black pepper to taste

2 tablespoons plain flour

2 oz (50 g) butter or vegetable oil

Put all the greens in a large bowl, mix well and stir in the beaten egg. Add the walnuts, salt and black pepper and gradually stir in the flour. Melt the butter or oil in a baking dish and add the vegetable mixture. Cover and bake in a preheated oven at 350° F (175° C, gas mark 4) for 45 minutes. Remove the cover and bake for a further 15 minutes. The top should be nicely browned.

Aubergine and cheese dish

4 medium aubergines, cut in
¼ in (6 mm) thick slices
4 fl oz (100 ml) vegetable oil
12 oz (350 g) cheese (e.g.
Cheddar, Mozzarella,
Gruyère, etc.) sliced
1 egg, beaten
8 oz (225 g) fresh tomatoes,
skinned and chopped, *or*
8 oz (225 g) tinned tomatoes,
drained and chopped

3 tablespoons tomato paste,
diluted with 3 tablespoons
water
½ medium onion, diced
salt and black pepper to taste

Salt the aubergines and set aside in a colander for 30 minutes. Rinse, drain and pat dry on absorbent paper. Fry the slices light brown on both sides in the vegetable oil. Layer the aubergine and cheese slices in a baking dish. Beat the remaining ingredients together and pour over the top. Bake uncovered in a preheated oven at 350° F (175° C, gas mark 4) for 20 minutes. Remove from the oven and serve.

Aubergine and egg casserole

4 medium aubergines, peeled
and sliced thinly
4 fl oz (100 ml) vegetable oil
juice of 2 lemons
4 oz (100 g) Parmesan or other
hard cheese, grated

2 cloves garlic, crushed
salt and black pepper to taste
4 eggs, separated

To make this soufflé-type dish, first salt the aubergine slices and set then aside in a colander for 30 minutes. Rinse, drain and pat them dry on absorbent paper. Fry them in most of the oil until browned and well softened. Mash the aubergines in a bowl and stir in the cheese, lemon juice and garlic. Season to taste with salt and black pepper. Beat the egg whites until very fluffy, and fold them into the beaten yolks. Fold this mixture into the aubergines and cheese. Transfer to a baking dish greased with the remaining oil and bake in a preheated oven at 350° F (175° C, gas mark 4) for 45 minutes. Serve with green salad and a bowl of yoghurt.

Aubergines in tomato sauce

4 medium aubergines, thickly
   sliced
12 oz (225 g) plain flour
6 fl oz (175 ml) water
2 eggs, beaten

salt and black pepper to taste
2 cloves garlic, finely chopped
about 1 pt (575 ml) tomato
   sauce (see p. 114)

Salt the aubergines, place them in a colander and leave for 30 minutes. Rinse, drain, and pat dry on absorbent paper. Beat the flour, water and eggs into a smooth batter. Dip the aubergine slices in the batter and then shallow fry them in hot oil on both sides until lightly browned. Layer the slices in a baking dish and season each layer with salt, black pepper and garlic. Just cover the aubergines with tomato sauce and bake them, covered, in a preheated oven at 350° F (175° C, gas mark 4) for 30 minutes. Serve hot or cold.

Aubergine and pastry roll

Serves 6

1 lb (450 g) plain flour
½ teaspoon salt
1 teaspoon baking powder
4 oz (100 g) butter or
   margarine, softened
6 fl oz (175 ml) yoghurt
1 large aubergine

2 fl oz (50 ml) tahini
2 cloves garlic, crushed
juice of 1 lemon
salt and pepper to taste
1 egg, beaten
sesame seeds

Sift the flour, salt and baking powder together. Rub in the butter or margarine and mix well. Add the yoghurt and knead the dough into a smooth ball. Place in the refrigerator for 30 minutes. Bake the aubergine in a preheated oven at 400° F (205° C, gas mark 5) for 30 minutes or until very tender and blackened. Peel and mash the pulp with the tahini, garlic, lemon juice and salt and pepper to taste. Roll out the dough into a rectangle about ½ in (1.3 cm) thick. Layer the aubergine filling down the long side of the dough rectangle and then roll the dough up like a carpet. It should roll up more than 2 layers thick. Brush with beaten egg and sprinkle with sesame seeds. Bake in a preheated oven at 350° F (175° C, gas mark 4) for 30 minutes or until nicely browned.

Fried aubergines with yoghurt

4 medium aubergines, sliced
8 fl oz (225 ml) yoghurt
2 cloves garlic, crushed
pinch of salt
2 fl oz (50 ml) olive oil or other
  vegetable oil

2 medium tomatoes, quartered
2 medium green peppers cored,
  seeded, sliced

Salt the aubergines, place in a colander and leave for 30 minutes. Rinse, drain, and pat dry on absorbent paper. Beat the garlic and a pinch of salt into the yoghurt and add a little water if it is very thick. Heat the oil in a heavy frying pan and fry the aubergine slices brown on both sides. You may need more oil. Put the slices in a moderate oven to keep warm. Fry the tomatoes and green peppers in the same frying pan, stirring all the time. As soon as the peppers are softened, tip the contents of the pan into a serving dish, put the aubergines on top, pour over the yoghurt and serve.

Baked courgettes

4 medium courgettes, washed
salt
4 eggs, lightly beaten
4 oz (100 g) grated cheese
  (Parmesan, Cheddar,
  Gruyère, etc.)

2 tablespoons chopped fresh
  parsley
4 oz (100 g) white flour
salt and black pepper to taste
2 oz (50 g) butter

Grate the unpeeled courgettes into a bowl, using a coarse grater. Sprinkle lightly with salt and set aside for 15 minutes. Meanwhile combine the eggs with the other ingredients except the butter and mix well. Preheat the oven to 350° F (175° C, gas mark 4). Wash the courgettes, allow them to drain and then squeeze well by hand to remove any excess liquid. Combine the egg mixture with the courgettes and pour into a buttered baking dish. Dot the top of the mixture with small knobs of butter and bake for 45 minutes.

Courgettes with garlic

4 medium courgettes
4 cloves garlic
1 teaspoon salt

1 teaspoon dried mint
2 fl oz (50 ml) olive oil
black pepper to taste

Cut the courgettes in half lengthwise and salt them. Leave in a colander for 30 minutes. Rinse, drain, and pat dry on absorbent paper. Crush the garlic, salt and mint into a paste. Put the oil into a heavy frying pan. Spread the garlic paste over the courgette halves and place them flesh side upwards in the pan. Sprinkle a little black pepper over them and cook over a moderate heat for 20 minutes or until the courgettes are tender.

Courgette rissoles

3 medium courgettes
salt
1 tablespoon flour
1 tablespoon chopped parsley
2 oz (50 g) cottage cheese

1 egg, lightly beaten
salt and black pepper to taste
breadcrumbs or flour
oil for deep frying

Thinly peel the courgettes and then grate them into a colander. Sprinkle with salt and leave for 15 minutes. Rinse under cold water. Press out any excess water and turn the courgettes into a mixing bowl. Add the remaining ingredients except the breadcrumbs and oil and mix well. Pinch off walnut-size pieces of the mixture and roll them in breadcrumbs or flour. Deep fry them in hot oil until crisp and golden.

Courgette and chick pea casserole

1 large onion, sliced
4 fl oz (100 ml) olive oil or
   other vegetable oil
8 oz (225 g) chick peas, cooked
4 medium courgettes, thickly
   sliced

1 tablespoon tomato paste
8 oz (225 ml) fresh or tinned
   tomatoes
salt and black pepper to taste

Sauté the onion in the oil in a heavy saucepan until just softened. Add the chick peas and courgettes, cover, and simmer for 15 minutes. Add the tomato paste and either fresh tomatoes, plus enough water to come halfway up the depth of vegetables, or tinned tomatoes plus enough of their liquid to reach the same point. Stir. Season to taste with salt and black pepper and simmer for 15 minutes. Serve hot or cold.

Moroccan potato casserole

This is a casserole which is especially good on cold winter days.

6 fl oz (175 ml) vegetable oil
1 medium red or green pepper,
   seeded, cored and diced
1 pt (575 ml) water
2 teaspoons ground cumin
1 small bunch parsley, chopped

5 cloves garlic, finely chopped
1½ lb (675 g) potatoes, peeled
   and quartered
rind of 1 lemon, grated
salt to taste

Heat the oil in a heavy casserole dish, add the diced pepper and lightly sauté. Carefully add half the water, stir in the cumin powder, the parsley and garlic and bring the mixture to the boil. Add the potatoes and lemon rind and return to the boil. Add the remaining water and salt to taste. Cook over a moderate heat until the potatoes are tender, and serve.

Fried Moroccan potatoes

1½ lb (675 g) potatoes, washed
   and peeled
2 tablespoons olive oil
1 small onion, diced, *or*
3 spring onions, chopped

2 cloves garlic, crushed
1 teaspoon ground cumin
4 oz (100 g) black olives, stoned
salt and black pepper to taste

Boil the potatoes until not quite tender and still firm. Cut them into about 1 in (2.5 cm) cubes. Heat the oil in a heavy frying pan and lightly sauté the onion and garlic. Add the potatoes, cumin and olives and stir fry over a gentle heat until the potatoes are tender and the olives very hot. Season to taste and serve.

Potato and tomato casserole

This dish is at its best when new potatoes and fresh red tomatoes are available.

2 medium onions, thinly sliced
2 tablespoons butter
1 lb (450 g) potatoes, scrubbed
   or peeled, and thinly sliced
1 lb (450 g) tomatoes, sliced
3 cloves garlic, crushed

10 fl oz (275 ml) vegetable
   stock
3 tablespoons chopped fresh
   parsley or mint
salt and pepper to taste

Preheat the oven to 400° F (205° C, gas mark 5). Melt the butter in a casserole dish and gently sauté the onion rings. Layer the potatoes on top, then the tomatoes. Crush the garlic over them, pour in the stock and add two-thirds of the fresh parsley or mint. Season to taste with salt and black pepper. Cover and bake for 35 to 45 minutes, or until the potatoes are tender. Serve garnished with the remaining herbs.

Carrots with caraway seeds

1 lb (450 g) carrots, peeled and sliced
2 tablespoons flour
salt and pepper to taste
2 tablespoons vegetable oil
8 oz (225 ml) yoghurt
1 teaspoon caraway seeds

Boil the carrots in salted water until almost tender but still firm. Then drain them and leave them until cool enough to pick up. Season the flour with salt and black pepper and toss the carrots in the mixture. Heat the oil in a heavy frying pan and fry the carrots on both sides until nicely browned. Meanwhile have the yoghurt gently warming up in a heavy pan. Transfer the carrots to a dish, pour the yoghurt over them and sprinkle with caraway seeds. Serve immediately as a side dish.

Cooked olives

2 tablespoons vegetable oil
6 cloves garlic, finely chopped
1 lb (450 g) green olives, stoned
pinch of cayenne
1 small bunch parsley, finely chopped
8 fl oz (225 ml) water
salt to taste
juice of 1 lemon
slices of lemon for garnishing

Sauté the garlic golden in the olive oil in a heavy pan. Add the olives, cayenne, parsley, water and salt to taste. Simmer uncovered for 30 minutes or until most of the liquid has evaporated. Stir in the lemon juice, adjust the seasoning, and serve garnished with slices of lemon as an appetizer or side dish.

Okra in oil

1 lb (450 g) okra, with stem ends removed	2 tablespoons chopped fresh parsley
4 fl oz (100 ml) mild vinegar	4 cloves garlic, crushed
4 fl oz (100 ml) olive oil	salt and black pepper to taste
2 medium onions, sliced	juice of ½ lemon
2 large tomatoes, quartered	4 fl oz (100 ml) water

Put the okra in a bowl, add the vinegar and leave to soak for 2 hours. Drain; reserve the vinegar for future use or discard it. Rinse the okra under cold water and drain again. Put half the oil in a heavy pan and lightly brown the onions. Add the tomatoes and cook until soft. Add the okra, parsley, garlic, salt and pepper to taste, lemon juice, water and remaining oil. Bring to the boil, reduce heat, cover and simmer for 30 minutes. Serve medium warm or cold.

Okra stew

1 lb (450 g) fresh or frozen okra, with stem ends removed	½ teaspoon ground coriander
	2 tablespoons tomato paste
	8 fl oz (225 ml) water
2 medium onions, sliced	salt and black pepper to taste
2 oz (50 g) butter	juice of 1 lemon

Melt the butter in a saucepan and sauté the onion light brown. Add the okra and sauté for 2 to 3 minutes. Add all the remaining ingredients except the lemon juice and mix well, bring to the boil, reduce heat, cover and simmer for 30 minutes. Sprinkle with lemon juice, and serve over rice, or noodles and rice (p. 79).

Cauliflower in avocado and tahini sauce

1 medium cauliflower, broken into large florets	salt to taste
	2 tablespoons sesame seeds, lightly toasted
juice of 1 lemon	1 small lettuce
1 large, ripe avocado	
8 fl oz (225 ml) tahini	

Put the cauliflower in a saucepan and just cover it with water. Add the lemon juice and cook until the cauliflower is just tender. Drain and leave to cool. Combine the avocado flesh and tahini and mix into a smooth sauce. Stir in salt to taste. Arrange the cauliflower on a bed of lettuce, pour over the sauce, sprinkle with sesame seeds, and serve.

Green beans in oil

A Turkish dish normally served cold. If you want to serve it hot use corn oil or butter in place of the olive oil. Any sort of fresh green beans may be used. If you do not have any wine available, substitute water.

4 tablespoons olive oil
1 large onion, finely chopped
2 large tomatoes, skinned and chopped
1 lb (450 g) green beans, washed, stringed and cut in half
2 cloves garlic, crushed

1 teaspoon sugar
4 fl oz (100 ml) dry white wine (optional)
water
salt to taste
juice of 1 lemon (if wine is not used)

Heat the oil in a heavy saucepan and lightly sauté the onion. Add the tomatoes and beans, mix well and sauté for a couple of minutes before adding the garlic, sugar and wine or water. Cover and simmer for 10 minutes. Add water just to cover, salt to taste and simmer for 45 minutes. Allow to cool, and serve sprinkled with lemon juice if wine has not been used.

Leeks in oil

Substitute 1 lb (450 g) of chopped leeks, white part only, for the green beans used in the recipe above.

Leek croquettes

This is an Israeli recipe. *Matzo* meal is required but if none is available substitute fine breadcrumbs.

1 lb (450 g) leeks, white part only, finely chopped
4 oz (100 g) *matzo* meal
2 eggs, beaten

1 tablespoon vegetable oil
salt and black pepper
oil for frying

Put the leeks in a pan, just cover them with water and simmer until very tender. Drain, and combine the leeks with the remaining ingredients. Mix well and add a little more *matzo* meal if the consistency is too soft. Chill the mixture and then form it into small croquettes. Fry them brown on both sides in hot oil.

Lebanese fried vegetables

½ head cauliflower, in small florets
1 large potato, peeled and cut in ¼ in (6 mm) rounds
1 medium aubergine, cut in ¼ in (6 mm) rounds, salted, rinsed and drained

1 medium courgette, cut in ½ in (1.3 cm) rounds
2 eggs, beaten
flour
oil for deep frying
fresh mint or parsley for garnishing

Heat the oil to the point at which it just starts to smoke. Dip the pieces of vegetable in the beaten egg, roll them in flour and deep fry until golden. Drain on absorbent paper, arrange in rows on a serving plate, and garnish with fresh mint or parsley. Serve with cucumber and yoghurt salad and pitta bread.

Stuffed vegetables (mishshi)

Stuffed aubergine boats

4 medium aubergines, stalks left on
3 large onions, sliced
4 cloves garlic, crushed
4 oz (100 g) butter or olive oil
14 oz (400 g) tinned tomatoes

salt and black pepper to taste
6 oz (175 g) cheese (e.g. Parmesan, Cheddar, Gruyère, etc.), grated
approximately 8 fl oz (225 ml) stock or water

Wash the aubergines complete with stalks, and make a deep slit from one end to the other without actually breaking open the ends. Press open the slit and sprinkle liberally with salt. Set the aubergines aside for 30 minutes. In a heavy saucepan, sauté the onions and garlic in half the butter or oil until soft and just browned. Drain the tomatoes, reserving the liquid, and add them to the onions and garlic. Season the mixture to taste with salt and black pepper and leave to cook over a low heat until the tomatoes have disintegrated.

Rinse out the aubergines and pat dry. Heat the remaining butter or oil in a heavy frying pan and fry the aubergines all over until they have softened but have not lost their shape. Preheat the oven to 350° F (175° C, gas mark 4). Pack the aubergines into a baking dish with the slits facing upwards. Combine the cheese with the onion and tomato mixture and stuff the aubergines with the result. Pour into the dish the reserved tomato juice and enough stock or water to come halfway up the sides of the aubergines. Bake for 45 minutes for until the aubergines are soft. Serve on rice with the cooking liquid spooned over.

Aubergines stuffed with rice

This is another version of the well-known Turkish dish *imam bayildi*, or 'The Imam Fainted'.

6 medium aubergines
6 fl oz (125 ml) olive oil or other vegetable oil
8 oz (225 g) long grain rice
2 medium onions, finely chopped
1 tablespoon pine nuts or chopped walnuts
2 medium tomatoes, chopped

1 tablespoon currants
1 tablespoon fresh herbs (e.g. parsley, dill or mint), *or*
1 teaspoon dried mixed herbs
8 fl oz (225 ml) water or stock
1 teaspoon sugar
salt and black pepper to taste
juice of 1 lemon

Cut the stem away from each of the aubergines, leaving the end intact. Cut a 2 in (5 cm) piece off the end of each and reserve them for plugging the stuffed aubergines later. With a spoon or sharp knife scoop out the pulp from the insides of the aubergines, leaving the shell intact and about ¼ to ½ in (6 mm to 1.3 cm) thick. Reserve the pulp for later use in stews, pureés, dips, etc. Salt the insides of the hollowed aubergines and set aside.

Cover the rice in boiling water and set aside until the water has cooled. Heat half the oil in a heavy frying pan and sauté the onion until golden. Drain the rice and add it to the onions, then add the pine nuts and stir well. Cover the pan and cook very gently for 20 minutes. Add the remaining ingredients except for the lemon juice and reserved oil and cook for another 15 minutes.

Rinse out the aubergines and fill with the rice stuffing. Pack them into a large saucepan and pour over the remaining oil. Add the lemon juice and just enough water to cover the aubergines. Cover the pan and gently simmer for 45 minutes or until the aubergines are very soft and tender. Remove from the heat, leave to cool, and serve.

Courgettes imam bayildi

Follow the previous recipe exactly, but replace the aubergines by courgettes. Hollow the courgettes out with an apple corer.

Aubergines stuffed with rice and chick peas

6 medium aubergines
4 oz (100 g) cooked chick peas, drained
4 oz (100 g) long grain rice, washed and drained
8 oz (225 g) tinned tomatoes, drained, *or*
8 oz (225 g) fresh tomatoes, skinned and chopped

2 medium onions, finely diced
1 teaspoon ground cinnamon
salt and black pepper to taste
8 oz (225 g) tomatoes, sliced
4 fl oz (100 ml) olive oil or other vegetable oil
water

Cut the stems away from the aubergines and halve them lengthwise. Hollow out the flesh from each half, leaving a shell about ½ in (1.3 cm) thick. Salt the inside and set aside for 30 minutes. The flesh can be chopped up, salted, fried and added to the filling when it is made, or it can be reserved for stews, soups, purées, etc.

Combine the chick peas, rice, tinned or chopped fresh tomatoes, onions and cinnamon and mix well. Season to taste with salt and black pepper. Rinse the aubergines and pat dry with a cloth or absorbent paper. Loosely pack them with the rice and chick pea mixture (remember that the rice will expand). Pour the oil into a baking dish and pack in the aubergines. Cover them with the tomato slices and add just enough water to the dish to cover the sides of the aubergines. Cover the dish and gently simmer on top of the stove or bake in a preheated oven at 350° F (175° C, gas mark 4) for 45 minutes or until the aubergines and rice are both tender. Serve as they are with yoghurt and salad as a main course, or cool and serve as a first course.

The chick peas in the recipe may be replaced by 2 oz (50 g) of chopped nuts or dried fruit or a mixture of both. If you decide to do this, increase the quantity of rice in the recipe to 6 oz (175 g).

Red or green peppers stuffed with spinach

4 medium peppers, red if possible
2 tablespoons olive oil
1 medium onion, diced
2 cloves garlic, crushed

1 lb (450 g) spinach, washed and finely chopped
8 oz (225 g) cooked rice
salt and black pepper to taste
water or stock

Cut the tops off the peppers and remove the seeds and pith. Heat the oil in a heavy frying pan and lightly sauté the whole peppers, turning them so that they are cooked all over. Remove and set aside. Sauté the onions and garlic in the same frying pan until just browned. Cook the spinach in a tiny amount of salted water until soft and wilted. Drain, and press out any excess moisture. Combine the onions, garlic, spinach, rice and salt and pepper to taste and stuff the peppers with this mixture. Put the tops on, pack the peppers tightly into a baking dish, and sprinkle them with a little stock or water. Bake in a preheated oven at 350° F (175° C, gas mark 4) for 30 minutes.

Rice-stuffed peppers

1 tablespoon olive oil or other vegetable oil
2 medium onions, diced
1 clove garlic, crushed
14 oz (400 g) tinned tomatoes
1 teaspoon dried basil

6 oz (175 g) long grain rice, uncooked
salt and black pepper to taste
4 large red or green peppers
water or stock

Sauté the onions and garlic in the oil until just browned. Drain the tomatoes and reserve the juice. Blend or crush the tomatoes and add to the onion and garlic. Stir in the basil and gently simmer for 10 minutes. Stir in the rice and salt and pepper to taste. Set aside. Cut the tops off the peppers and remove the pith and seeds. Reserve the tops. Fill the peppers two-thirds full with the rice mixture and pack tightly into a baking dish. Put the tops on them and pour the reserved tomato juice into the dish. Add water or stock to bring the level halfway up the sides of the peppers, cover and bake in a preheated oven at 350° F (175° C, gas mark 4) for 45 minutes or until the rice and peppers are tender.

Peppers stuffed with lentils and bulgar wheat

4 large green or red peppers
4 tablespoons olive oil
1 medium onion, diced
½ teaspoon allspice
½ teaspoon ground cinnamon
½ teaspoon sugar
8 oz (225 g) cooked lentils

8 oz (225 g) bulgar wheat,
  washed and drained
2 tablespoons chopped fresh
  parsley
2 oz (50 g) walnuts, chopped
water or stock

Cut the tops off the peppers and remove the pith and seeds. Reserve the tops. Put half the oil in a heavy saucepan and sauté the onion, add the allspice, cinnamon and sugar and stir well. Add the lentils and bulgar wheat and sauté, stirring often, for 5 minutes. Pack this mixture into the peppers. Brush the peppers with some of the remaining oil and pack tightly into a baking dish. Put the tops on, and sprinkle over them the chopped walnuts and a little more olive oil. Pour in water or stock to surround the peppers halfway up the sides. Cover and bake in a preheated oven at 350° F (175° C, gas mark 4) for 30 to 35 minutes or until the peppers are tender.

Courgettes stuffed with lentils and bulgar wheat

4 medium courgettes, halved
  lengthwise
4 tablespoons olive oil or other
  vegetable oil
1 medium onion, finely diced
2 cloves garlic, crushed
1 teaspoon allspice

8 oz (225 g) lentils, split or
  whole, cooked
8 oz (225 g) bulgar wheat,
  washed and drained
salt and black pepper to taste
2 oz (50 g) walnuts, chopped

Scoop the flesh out of the courgette halves, leaving a shell ½ to ¾ in (1.3 to 2 cm) thick. Reserve the pulp. Cover the shells in salted boiling water and leave for 3 to 4 minutes. Drain and set aside. Heat half the oil in a heavy saucepan and sauté the onion and garlic until just softened. Add the chopped reserved pulp and all the remaining ingredients except the walnuts and the rest of the oil. Stir and cook gently for 10 minutes. Stuff the courgette shells with the mixture and pack them into a baking dish. Brush with the remaining olive oil and sprinkle chopped walnuts over the top. Cover and bake in a preheated oven at 350° F (175° C, gas mark 4) for 25 minutes. Serve hot or cold.

The bulgar wheat may be replaced by 8 oz (225 g) cooked rice.

Stuffed courgettes with apricots

4 medium courgettes, sliced
  lengthwise
3 tablespoons olive oil
1 medium onion, diced
8 oz (225 g) long grain rice
8 fl oz (225 ml) water
1 tablespoon tomato paste
½ teaspoon sugar

1 teaspoon ground cinnamon
salt and black pepper to taste
16 fl oz (450 ml) water
1 tablespoon honey
8 oz (225 g) dried apricots,
  diced
juice of 1 lemon

Scoop the pulp out of the courgettes, leaving shells about ¾ in (2 cm) thick. Chop up the scooped-out pulp. Heat the oil in a heavy pan, add the onion and courgette pulp, and sauté until the onion is just soft. Add the rice, water, tomato paste, sugar, cinnamon and salt and black pepper to taste. Bring to the boil, reduce to simmer, and cook for 15 minutes with occasional stirring. Meanwhile cover the courgette shells in boiling salted water and leave for 2 to 3 minutes. Drain them, stuff them with the rice mixture, and set aside. Combine the water, honey and apricots and boil until the apricots are completely softened. Preheat the oven to 350° F (175° C, gas mark 4). Spoon into a heavy casserole dish half the apricots and juice, place the stuffed courgettes on top, and pour over the remaining apricots and juice. Sprinkle with the lemon juice and bake for 30 minutes or until the courgettes are soft and tender. Serve hot or cold.

Stuffed cabbage leaves

This is a popular cheap dish which is basically the same idea as stuffed vine leaves (p. 26).

8 oz (225 g) long grain rice,
  washed and drained
1 medium onion, finely diced
2 tablespoons tomato paste
2 cloves garlic, crushed
2 tablespoons finely chopped
  fresh parsley

1 teaspoon ground cinnamon
salt and black pepper to taste
1 medium cabbage
olive oil or other vegetable oil
  to taste
water or stock
juice of 1 lemon

Combine the first seven ingredients and mix well. Set aside. Wash the cabbage and trim off the stalk. If you can, strip off the leaves from the cabbage intact and cut out any hard central leaf stalks. Wash them again and then dip them, a few at a time, in boiling salted water until they become wilted and pliable. If it proves difficult to remove the leaves from the cabbage without them splitting, put the whole cabbage into a pan of boiling salted water and leave for 3 to 4 minutes. Lift the cabbage out, drain it, and then peel off the leaves. Trim off the hard central leaf stalks, cut the large leaves in 2, and proceed as above.

Put a tablespoon of the prepared stuffing mixture into the centre of each leaf. Fold the leaf corners into the centre and roll up, making a neat finger shape. Repeat this until all the filling is used up. Now line a large saucepan with unused or torn leaves, which helps to prevent the stuffed leaves sticking to the bottom. Lay the stuffed leaves on top, arranging each at an angle so that it does not come into contact with the others. Sprinkle with the olive oil. Cover with water or stock and add the lemon juice and a little salt. Cover the pan and cook gently for about 1 hour or until the leaves and rice are tender. Serve hot or cold.

General-purpose fillings for vegetables

Use either of the two fillings given below or one of the fillings given in the previous recipes for stuffing any suitable vegetable. Specific details of how to prepare onions, tomatoes, marrows, potatoes and artichokes for stuffing and cooking follow.

Rice and nut filling

This recipe provides enough filling for preparing stuffed vegetables for 4 to 6 people

2 tablespoons vegetable oil or butter
1 medium onion, diced
8 oz (225 g) rice, washed
2 oz (50 g) chopped nuts (e.g. walnuts, pistachio or whole pine nuts)

2 oz (50 g) currants
12 fl oz (350 ml) water or stock
½ teaspoon allspice
salt and black pepper to taste

Sauté the onion until golden in the oil or butter in a heavy saucepan. Add the rice and nuts and sauté, stirring, for 2 to 3 minutes. Add the remaining ingredients, stir well, and bring to the boil. Reduce the heat, cover and simmer for 20 minutes or until the rice is cooked and all the liquid is absorbed.

Rice and chick pea filling

This recipe provides enough filling for stuffing vegetables for 4 to 6 people

2 tablespoons olive oil or other vegetable oil	8 oz (225 g) cooked chick peas
1 medium onion, diced, *or*	1 tablespoon chopped fresh mint or parsley, *or*
1 bunch spring onions, chopped	1 teaspoon dried mint or parsley
2 medium leeks, white only, finely chopped	salt and black pepper to taste
8 oz (225 g) cooked rice	

Sauté the onions and leeks in the oil until soft and just browned. Add to the other ingredients and mix well.

Stuffing specific vegetables

Stuffed onions

4 to 6 large onions, peeled   juice of 1 lemon
selected filling

Cook the onions in a small amount of water over a low heat for 20 minutes. Drain and reserve the liquid. Cut a slice off the stem end of each onion and scoop out the centres, leaving a moderately thick wall. Stuff the onions with the selected filling. Set aside. Chop up the centres and place in a baking dish along with the reserved liquid and the juice of 1 lemon. Pack the stuffed onions into the dish, cover and bake in a preheated oven at 350° F (175° C, gas mark 4) for 1 hour or simmer, covered, over a low heat on top of the oven for the same time.

Stuffed tomatoes

8 to 12 or more medium tomatoes	2 oz (50 g) chopped nuts
selected filling	2 tablespoons olive oil
	salt and black pepper to taste

Cut ¼ to ½ in (6 mm to 1.3 cm) tops off the tomatoes and reserve them. Carefully scoop out the tomato pulp, leaving a ½ in (1.3 cm) shell. Sprinkle the inside with salt and black pepper and set aside. Chop the pulp and add to the filling. Stuff the tomatoes and brush them all over with olive oil. Put them in a shallow baking dish and put the tops on. Bake in a preheated oven at 350° F (175° C, gas mark 4) for 20 minutes. Serve hot or cold.

Stuffed marrows

2 to 3 medium marrows, cut lengthwise in 2	1 small green pepper, seeded, cored and diced
selected filling	2 tablespoons chopped fresh parsley
2 tablespoons vegetable oil	
2 medium tomatoes, chopped	salt and black pepper to taste
1 small onion, diced	juice of 1 lemon

Put the marrows in a pan of salted boiling water and cook until the pulp is softened. Drain, and scoop out the pulp, leaving a thick shell. Stuff the marrows with the selected filling and set aside.

Put the oil in a flameproof baking dish and add all the remaining ingredients except the lemon juice. Sauté and stir until the onions are softened. Lay the stuffed marrows on this sauce and cover the dish. Bake in a preheated oven at 350° F (175° C, gas mark 4) for 45 minutes. Serve sprinkled with lemon juice.

Stuffed potatoes

8 to 12 medium potatoes, peeled	2 large tomatoes, sliced water
selected filling	

Hollow out each potato with a sharp knife or spoon or apple corer, leaving a shell about ½ in (1.3 cm) thick with one end intact. Stuff with the selected filling and arrange the potatoes upright in a greased baking dish. Cover the tops with tomato slices and add enough water just to reach the tops of the potatoes. Bake in a preheated oven at 400° F (205° C, gas mark 5) for 35 minutes or longer until the potatoes are tender. This dish is normally served with rice.

Stuffed artichokes

Allow 2 globe artichokes per person for a main meal, and 1 per person for starters.

globe artichokes	6 fl oz (175 ml) water
selected filling	juice of 1 lemon
1 tablespoon vegetable oil	salt and pepper to taste

Remove the outer, coarse leaves of the artichokes, leaving only the inner, tender ones. Trim these leaves with scissors to a height of about 2 in (5 cm). Remove the fuzzy choke with a spoon or fork to reveal the heart, and cut away any thorny inner leaves. Trim off the bottoms of the artichokes. Store the prepared artichokes in a bowl of water, mixed with a squeeze of lemon juice, until they are all

ready. Stuff the hearts with the selected filling and place the artichokes in a large pan. Mix the oil, water and lemon juice and season
to taste with salt and black pepper. Pour this into the pan, bring the
liquid to the boil, reduce heat, cover and simmer for 1 hour or until
the artichokes are tender. Add more water if necessary.

SAUCES

The following sauces can be served with vegetable or rice dishes, with salads, or just on their own with bread. Stuffed vegetables baked in tomato sauce are particularly good, and aubergine sauce makes use of the flesh from aubergines that have been hollowed out for stuffing. When making tahini sauces always blend water (if called for) with the tahini before the addition of other liquids. When heating yoghurt sauces always stir constantly and be careful not to burn them.

Tomato sauce

2 oz (50 g) butter or vegetable
oil
1 medium onion, finely diced
4 cloves garlic, crushed
2 lb (900 g) fresh or tinned
tomatoes
1 medium green pepper,
seeded, cored and diced

2 teaspoons crushed oregano
2 tablespoons chopped fresh
parsley
1 bay leaf
salt and pepper to taste

Melt the butter in a heavy saucepan or pour in the oil, and fry the onions in this pan over a low heat until soft. Skin fresh tomatoes by dropping them in boiling water for a minute or two, then lift them out and peel off the skin. Alternatively use tinned tomatoes plus the juice. In either case chop the tomatoes into small pieces. Add the garlic, tomatoes and green pepper to the onions, stir well and simmer for 10 minutes. Add the herbs and season to taste with salt and black pepper. Simmer a further 10 minutes and allow to cool. Store in airtight jars, and pour a thin film of oil over the top of the sauce before screwing on the lid.

Quick tomato sauce

½ medium onion, finely diced
1 tablespoon vegetable oil
3 tablespoons tomato paste

10 fl oz (275 ml) water
pinch of sugar
salt and black pepper to taste

Sauté the onion in the oil until well softened. Stir in the tomato paste, water, sugar and seasoning. Mix well and bring to the boil. Remove from the heat, and it is ready.

Tomato paste

1 lb (450 g) tomatoes
½ teaspoon dried basil
1 tablespoon butter

1 clove garlic, crushed
salt and pepper to taste

Skin the tomatoes as described in the tomato sauce recipe. Now chop them finely and gently simmer them in the butter with the remaining ingredients until the mixture thickens to a purée consistency. Cool and use.

Aubergine sauces

Instead of whole aubergines, the flesh from aubergines that have been hollowed out for stuffing may be used in these recipes.

Aubergine cream sauce

2 to 3 medium aubergines
2 oz (50 g) butter
3 tablespoons flour
8 fl oz (225 ml) single cream

2 oz (50 g) grated cheese
salt to taste
grated peel of ½ a lemon

Slit the aubergines lengthwise and sprinkle salt in the cut. Set aside for 30 minutes, then rinse and drain. Place the aubergines in a preheated oven at 400° F (205° C, gas mark 5) for 20 minutes. Peel off the skin. Alternatively hold the aubergines, impaled one at a time on a skewer, over a gas flame and singe them all over until the skin bubbles and flakes off easily. Chop the aubergine flesh into small pieces.

Melt the butter in a heavy pan, stir in the flour, and cook, stirring, for 3 to 4 minutes. Add the aubergine flesh and beat to make a smooth mixture. Stir in the single cream and cheese and gently simmer, stirring, until the cheese is melted. Add salt to taste, mix in the lemon rind, and serve hot with vegetables.

If you use uncooked aubergine flesh rather than whole cooked aubergines, salt the flesh first, chop, rinse and then fry in a little butter before using it in the above recipe.

Aubergines and tomato sauce

2 to 3 medium aubergines	1 lb (450 g) tomatoes, skinned
2 oz (50 g) butter	and chopped
1 medium onion, finely diced	salt and black pepper to taste
4 cloves garlic, crushed	water

Salt and skin the aubergines as described in the previous recipe. Chop up the flesh and fry with the onion in the butter until lightly browned. Add the garlic, tomatoes, seasoning and water to moisten. Simmer until soft and mushy. If you plan to bake vegetables in this sauce dilute it with water first.

Tahini sauce

2 cloves garlic, crushed	4 fl oz (100 ml) water
1 teaspoon salt	juice of 2 lemons
4 fl oz (100 ml) tahini	

Mash the garlic with the salt in a bowl. Slowly beat in the tahini, water and lemon juice in that order. Blend well, using an electric blender if you like. For a thicker or thinner sauce use less or more water and lemon juice respectively.

This sauce is excellent just on its own with bread, or as a salad dressing. Also serve it with rice and vegetable dishes and as a dip for *mezze*.

Tahini and parsley sauce

Prepare the tahini sauce as described above and then stir in a small bunch of chopped parsley.

Tahini and walnut sauce

Follow the tahini sauce recipe above but crush 4 oz (100 g) walnuts with the garlic and salt. This sauce is delicious with lightly sautéed or boiled vegetables.

Yoghurt sauce with mint

1 clove garlic
1 teaspoon salt
2 teaspoons dried mint, *or*
3 tablespoons finely chopped
   fresh mint

2 oz (50 g) butter
1 pt (575 ml) yoghurt
1 egg, beaten
4 fl oz (100 ml) water

Crush the garlic, salt and mint together and sauté the mixture in the butter for 2 to 3 minutes. Set aside. Beat the yoghurt, egg and water together for 2 minutes and then stir the mixture in a heavy pan over a moderate heat for 10 minutes. Add the garlic and mint and continue cooking and stirring for another 10 minutes, before serving. The mixture should not come to the boil at any time.

Garlic sauce

4 cloves garlic
1 teaspoon salt

2 tablespoons olive oil
juice of 1 lemon

Crush the garlic and salt together in a bowl. Add the olive oil drop by drop, whisking all the time. Repeat with the lemon juice. Serve with salads or vegetables.

Garlic egg sauce

The ingredients are as for garlic sauce, plus 1 beaten egg. Crush the garlic and salt together in a bowl. Gradually add the egg, lemon juice and olive oil in that order, beating all the time. Continue beating until it becomes quite thick.

Garlic and walnut sauce

4 cloves garlic
1 teaspoon salt
2 tablespoon breadcrumbs,
   dampened with a little water

4 oz (100 g) walnuts, finely
   chopped or ground
2 tablespoons olive oil
juice of 1 lemon

Crush the garlic and salt together in a bowl. Add the breadcrumbs and chopped walnuts to the garlic and salt and then crush the mixture into a paste. Add the olive oil drop by drop, whisking all the time. Repeat with the lemon juice. The sauce is now ready, and is very good with aubergine and courgette dishes.

Lemon and egg sauce

2 eggs
juice of 1 lemon

2 tablespoons milk or stock
salt and black pepper to taste

Beat the eggs until light and frothy. Gradually beat in the lemon juice, milk or stock and season to taste with salt and black pepper. Add this sauce to cooking vegetable dishes and soups. It is also very good lightly beaten into cooked rice.

Creamy lemon and egg sauce

2 teaspoons cornflour, blended
   with 2 tablespoons water
6 fl oz (175 ml) stock

2 eggs, separated
juice of 2 lemons
salt

Stir the cornflour into the stock and bring to the boil. Allow to cool a little, beat the egg whites stiffly and beat in the egg yolks. Continue beating and gradually add the lemon juice. Now stir in the hot thickened stock to form a creamy sauce. Season with salt. Serve hot over vegetables or rice dishes.

Wine sauce

This sauce is unusual in that it contains wine. However, despite the alcohol, it does have a real Middle Eastern flavour to it.

2 medium onions, diced
2 cloves garlic, crushed
3 tablespoons olive oil
½ teaspoon thyme
1 bay leaf

1 tablespoon chopped parsley
salt and black pepper to taste
juice of 1 lemon
6 fl oz (150 ml) dry white wine
6 fl oz (150 ml) water

Sauté the onion and garlic in the oil until softened. Add the thyme, bay leaf, parsley and salt and black pepper to taste. Stir well and add the lemon juice, wine and water. Simmer uncovered over a low heat for 20 minutes. Serve hot or cold over vegetables or use as a marinade.

EGG DISHES

On special occasions and feast days, boiled eggs dyed in different colours are served along with other more exotic dishes as symbols of the potential and mystery of life. On ordinary days yellow-coloured boiled eggs seasoned with spices such as cumin are sold as snacks by street vendors to hungry passers-by. Eggs, with their shells scrubbed, are added whole to stews so that during the long cooking time the flavour of the stew will penetrate the shell. Omelettes and pancakes are as popular as in the West, although the Middle Eastern omelettes called *eggah* or *kuku* are thicker than their Western counterparts.

Browned hard-boiled eggs (hamindas)

In this traditional recipe, popular during festivals, the eggs are prepared by long cooking over a very low heat. Eggs cooked in this way have a delicate, distinctive flavour very different from an ordinary hard-boiled egg.

6 large fresh eggs
1 tablespoon oil

¼ teaspoon pepper
¼ teaspoon salt

Put the eggs in a saucepan, cover with water, add the oil, salt and pepper and simmer, covered, over a very low heat for 8 to 10 hours or overnight. Alternatively put the ingredients into a baking dish and bake at 200° F (95° C, gas mark ¼) overnight. Sometimes old coffee grains are added to the cooking water to make the eggs even browner.

Hard-boiled eggs with spices

Hard-boiled eggs are peeled and served with small bowls of salt, ground cinnamon, ground coriander and ground cumin to dip the eggs into. Alternatively the salt and spices can be mixed beforehand using equal quantities of salt and each spice.

Some times the peeled hard-boiled eggs are fried in a hot shallow oil before serving. This is the way Egyptian street vendors sell them.

Eggs on a straw carpet

4 eggs
2 tablespoons olive oil
thyme, salt and pepper to taste

Carefully break the eggs into a bowl, keeping the yolks whole. Heat the oil in a heavy frying pan. Slip the eggs gently but quickly into the hot oil (the oil may splutter a bit, so be careful). Cook until the egg whites becomes crisp and golden brown (this is the straw carpet). Season to taste with crushed thyme, salt and pepper.

Poached eggs in yoghurt

The Western palate takes some time to get used to the idea of this dish. It is in fact surprisingly good and looks interesting. Serve as a light meal or as a starter.

16 fl oz (450 ml) yoghurt   2 tablespoons butter
2 cloves garlic, crushed   1 teaspoon paprika
4 eggs   salt and black pepper to taste

Beat the yoghurt and garlic together and divide into 4 individual bowls. Poach the eggs in an egg poacher until the whites are set but the yolks still soft. Melt the butter and stir in the paprika. Slip a hot poached egg into each bowl of yoghurt, pour over some paprika and melted butter, and season to taste with salt and black pepper. Serve immediately.

Little omelettes

This is an Armenian dish, traditionally served at Easter but good at any time.

4 eggs
1 bunch parsley, finely chopped
1 bunch spring onions, finely chopped

1 clove garlic, crushed
salt and black pepper to taste
4 fl oz (100 ml) vegetable oil

Beat the eggs and stir in all the other ingredients except the oil. Heat the oil in a heavy frying pan and drop in tablespoonsful of the egg mixture. Fill the pan but carefully keep each tablespoon of mixture separate from the next. Turn the little omelettes to brown both sides and remove them from the pan. Continue until all the mixture has been cooked. Serve hot or cold.

Iranian vegetable omelette (kuku)

The Iranian *kuku* is that country's version of the Middle Eastern *eggah* (see p. 124).

2 oz (50 g) butter
1 medium leek, white only, chopped
1 medium onion, finely sliced
1 medium potato, peeled and finely sliced
2 tomatoes, thinly sliced

1 medium green pepper, seeded and thinly sliced
1 teaspoon dried basil
2 tablespoons chopped fresh parsley
salt and black pepper to taste
8 eggs, beaten

Melt half the butter in a large, heavy frying pan, add the onion, leek and potatoes and sauté until tender. Press the mixture down on to the bottom of the pan and arrange over the top the tomato, green pepper slices, basil, parsley and salt and black pepper to taste. Dot the top with pieces of the remaining butter. Pour the eggs over, cover the top of the pan with a lid or large plate and simmer over a low heat until the egg is set all the way through. Invert on to a serving dish. Alternatively, after the eggs have been added, the mixture can be turned into an oiled baking dish, covered, and baked in a preheated oven at 350° F (175° C, gas mark 4) for 45 minutes. Remove the cover for the last 15 minutes.

Chatchouka (eggs with tomatoes)

This is a dish of North African origin, said to be the basis of the Spanish omelette. It is now widely popular in the Middle East.

2 tablespoons butter or
   vegetable oil
2 medium green peppers,
   seeded and thinly sliced
½ to 1 small hot chilli pepper,
   chopped (optional)
2 medium onions, diced

2 cloves garlic, crushed
1 lb (450 g) small tomatoes,
   halved
salt and black pepper to taste
6 eggs
parsley for garnishing (optional)

In a heavy frying pan sauté in butter or oil the green peppers, chilli pepper, onion and garlic until the onion is softened. Add the tomatoes, season to taste with salt and black pepper and cook gently until the tomatoes are very soft. Adjust the seasoning. Break the eggs over the surface and stir gently to break the yolks. Cook until set and season again. Serve on toast or with rice. Garnish with fresh parsley if you wish.

Turkish omelette

Serves 2 to 4

2 tablespoons butter or
   margarine
8 oz to 1 lb (225 to 450 g) of
   any single vegetable or
   combination of the following
   vegetables: potatoes, diced;
   onion, sliced; leeks, sliced;
   tomatoes, chopped; green
   peppers, seeded, cored and
   sliced

4 eggs, beaten
salt and black pepper to taste
parsley for garnishing
paprika
lemon juice to taste

Melt the butter or margarine in a heavy frying pan and sauté the vegetables over moderate heat until just softened. Beat the eggs with salt and black pepper to taste and pour into the pan. Keep folding the edges of the omelette over and then surrounding them with liquid, uncooked egg. When all the egg is set but not too firm fold the omelette in half. Serve garnished with parsley and sprinkled with paprika and lemon juice to taste.

Avocado omelette

Serves 1

flesh of ½ medium ripe
  avocado
2 eggs, beaten
salt to taste

parsley for garnishing
thick lemon slices for
  garnishing

Beat the avocado flesh and eggs together to form a smooth mixture.
Salt to taste. Pour the mixture into a lightly greased pan and cook
until golden on both sides. Serve garnished with the parsley and
lemon slices.

Walnut omelette

6 eggs, beaten
4 oz (100 g) walnuts, chopped
2 oz (50 g) currants, washed
1 tablespoon chopped chives,
  spring onions or onion

½ teaspoon turmeric or saffron
4 tablespoons breadcrumbs
salt and black pepper to taste
oil for frying

For this Iraqi recipe, combine all the ingredients except the oil and
mix well. Heat the oil in a large, heavy frying pan and pour in the
egg mixture. Cook over a low heat until the omelette sets. Turn
and brown the other side. Serve immediately.

Eggah

This Middle Eastern omelette, is firm, thick and well filled, not at
all like a European omelette. *Eggah* is served like a pie, cut into
wedges, or into squares if straight-edged (for hors d'oeuvres it can
be cut into very small pieces). Serve as a main dish with salad, or
as hors d'oeuvres.

Eggs with spinach

2 oz (50 g) butter or margarine
1 medium onion, finely sliced
1 lb (450 g) spinach, washed
  and chopped

4 eggs
salt and black pepper to taste

Sauté the onion in the butter until just soft in a flameproof baking dish on top of the stove. Add the spinach and cook over a low heat until wilted. Spread the spinach evenly over the bottom of the dish and carefully break the 4 eggs separately on top of it. Cover the dish and gently cook until the eggs are set. Season and serve immediately.

Vegetable eggah

3 oz (75 g) butter or margarine
1 lb (450 g) of any single
  vegetable or combination
  from the following:
  courgettes, thinly sliced;
  potatoes, cooked and sliced;
  mushrooms, cleaned and
  sliced; aubergines, sliced,
  salted and drained; beetroots,
  cooked and sliced; spinach,
  washed and chopped; leeks,
  washed and sliced; onions,
  thinly sliced

2 cloves garlic, crushed
2 tablespoons chopped fresh
  parsley
6 eggs, lightly beaten
salt and black pepper to taste

Melt 2 oz (50 g) of the butter in a heavy frying pan. Add the selected vegetable or vegetables (add them in stages if one vegetable obviously cooks faster than another) and garlic and sauté over a moderate heat until they are just tender. Transfer to a bowl and set aside. Clean out the frying pan, or use a second pan. Beat together the eggs, parsley and salt and black pepper and stir the mixture into the bowl containing the cooked vegetables. Melt the remaining butter in the frying pan and pour in the egg and vegetable mixture. Cook slowly for 15 minutes. Brown the top of the *eggah* lightly under a grill.

Baked Tunisian eggah

2 oz (50 g) butter or olive oil
3 to 4 cloves garlic, crushed
2 medium courgettes, thinly
  sliced
1 medium onion, thinly sliced
2 medium green or red peppers,
  seeded cored and sliced
1 lb (450 g) tomatoes, quartered

¼ to ½ teaspoon cayenne or
  harissa (see Glossary)
½ teaspoon ground cumin
½ teaspoon ground coriander
½ teaspoon ground cinnamon
pinch of nutmeg
salt and black pepper to taste
6 eggs, lightly beaten

Preheat the oven to 350° F (175° C, gas mark 4). Sauté the garlic, courgettes and onion in the butter or oil in a heavy frying pan until the onion is softened. Add the peppers, tomatoes, spices and salt and black pepper to taste. Stir and sauté for 2 to 3 minutes. Now add just enough water to cover and cook over a lot heat for 20 minutes or until most of the liquid has evaporated or been absorbed. Transfer this mixture to a lightly greased baking dish and stir in the eggs. Adjust the seasoning, and bake for 40 to 45 minutes. Remove the cover for the last 15 minutes. The top should be nicely browned.

Syrian stuffed pancakes

Syrian pancakes are small and often stuffed with a local cheese similar to cottage cheese. They are popular at breakfast with eggs, olives and fruit.

Serves 6 to 8

1 tablespoon butter, softened
8 fl oz (225 ml) milk
1 egg
8 oz (225 g) plain flour, sifted

oil for frying
6 oz (175 g) cottage cheese
honey or syrup

Combine the butter, milk, egg and flour and gently mix into a batter. Lightly oil a heavy frying pan and heat it over a moderate flame. Drop dessertspoonfuls of batter into the pan to form small circular pancakes and fry them on one side only. Remove from the pan and place 1 teaspoon of cottage cheese in the centre of each on the uncooked side. Fold the pancakes in half and press the edges together. Return the stuffed pancakes to the pan and brown on both sides. Transfer to a serving dish. Put equal parts of honey or syrup and water in the pan, warm and mix. Pour this over the pancakes before serving.

Yoghurt pancakes

2 eggs, separated
1 tablespoon sugar
8 fl oz (225 ml) yoghurt
1 tablespoon butter, melted
6 oz (175 g) plain flour, sifted

1 teaspoon baking powder
pinch of salt
oil for frying
honey

Beat the egg yolks and mix them with the sugar, yoghurt and butter. Combine the flour, baking powder and salt and gradually stir into the yoghurt mixture. Beat the egg whites stiff and fold them into the mixture. Lightly oil and heat a heavy frying pan and drop tablespoonsful of the batter into it. Fry the pancakes light brown on both sides and serve with honey.

Armenian pancakes

The batter for these pancakes is much stiffer than normal and more like a dough. The pancakes can be served sweet or savoury.

Serves 6

1 egg, beaten
4 fl oz (100 ml) water
1 tablespoon butter, melted
10 oz (275 g) plain flour, sifted
1 teaspoon baking powder

pinch of salt
butter for frying
sugar or honey (for sweet
  pancakes only)

Combine thoroughly the egg, water and butter. Mix the flour, baking powder and salt and gradually stir this mixture into the wet ingredients. Knead well by hand to form a smooth dough. Pinch off walnut-size pieces of dough and roll into circles of about 6 in (15 cm) diameter. Heat a small amount of butter in a heavy frying pan and fry the pancakes brown on both sides. Add more butter as needed. Serve hot with sugar or honey or with a savoury spread.

Middle Eastern crêpes (ataif)

Ataif are the *crêpes* of the Middle East – paper-thin pancakes with a variety of fillings. The most popular is *eishta*, a type of clotted cream made traditionally from buffaloes' milk. Whipped or clotted cream can be substituted.

Serves 6

10 oz (275 g) plain flour, sifted
2 teaspoons granulated sugar
2 eggs, lightly beaten
1 tablespoon rosewater
12 fl oz (350 ml) milk

2 tablespoons butter, melted
vegetable oil for frying
4 oz (100 g) nuts, chopped
whipped cream

In a blender or mixing bowl combine the flour, sugar, eggs, rose-water, milk and butter and beat into a smooth batter. Put in the refrigerator for 1 hour. Mix again, and it's ready for use.

Barely cover the bottom of a large, heavy frying pan with oil and heat until hot but not smoking. Spoon in a small amount of batter and tilt the pan to coat the bottom completely. Cook until the edges start to brown then turn the *crêpe* over and cook the other side until nicely browned. Remove the *crêpe* and repeat until all the batter is used up.

Stack the cooked pancakes in a moderately warm oven if desired. Store in a refrigerator if they are not to be used right away. Spread a tablespoon of cream and some nuts on each pancake. Roll up and serve garnished with more cream.

SAVOURY AND SWEET PASTRIES

Pastries of all shapes and sizes and with all kinds of fillings are very popular in the Middle East. The savoury ones are served hot or cold as hors d'oeuvres, snacks, buffet dishes or party food. The shapes and fillings depend on local custom and, if it's for a celebration, the particular occasion involved. Ordinary shortcrust and puff pastry are used as well as the more popular *fila* pastry. Cheese, eggs, spinach and nuts in various combinations are common fillings. Sweet pastries are just as popular as savoury ones. They are sold in cafés, from market stalls and in bakeries, and are served to visitors at the slightest excuse since the host probably has just as sweet a tooth as his guest. Baklava and *kadayif* ('Shredded Wheat cakes') are typical sweet pastries and will be familiar to anyone who has eaten in Greek restaurants. They are made from a *fila* or *kadayif* pastry stuffed with a filling, normally of crushed nuts, and then baked and while still hot soaked in a honey or sugar syrup.

It is most confusing to attempt to distinguish the various pastries by name, since in one region or country the same pastry may have a different name from the one it is called in another region or country. Instead, I have identified the most common combinations of fillings and pastries and given recipes for these, together with their most common name.

Savoury pastries

Filled savoury pastries are some of the most interesting of Middle Eastern foods. They are made in a wide variety of shapes and sizes and from various types of pastry dough. The non-meat fillings are usually cheese- or spinach-based, or less often cooked vegetables.

To simplify matters I have decided to concentrate on the enormous selection of *boerek*-style pastries of Turkish origin, which include most of the types of pastries common to the Middle East.

Recipes for the various fillings are given first, followed by recipes for four popular pastry doughs – shortcrust, flaky, *fila* and *sumboosak*. The way that each particular dough is traditionally cut out, filled and baked is described too. The quantities given for pastry doughs and fillings will make approximately 30 small pastries.

The quantities given in the recipes will provide enough filling to use up a pastry dough made from 1 lb/450 g of flour or up to 1 lb/450 g of premade, shop bought *fila* pastry.

Cheese fillings

Recipe 1

1 lb (450 g) hard cheese, grated
2 eggs, beaten
pinch of salt (if the cheese is not
  salty)

1 small bunch parsley, finely
  chopped

Combine the ingredients and mix well.

Recipe 2

1 lb (450 g) feta cheese,
  crumbled, *or*
12 oz (350 g) feta cheese,
  crumbled, plus 4 oz (100 g)
  Parmesan, grated, mixed
  together

2 eggs, separated
2 tablespoons chopped fresh
  mint or parsley
pinch of salt (if the cheese is not
  salty)
black pepper to taste

Mix the cheese, egg yolks (use the whites for glazing), herbs and salt, season to taste with black pepper and beat until well blended.

Recipe 3

4 oz (100 g) cream cheese
6 oz (150 g) cottage cheese
4 oz (100 g) Swiss cheese (e.g.
  Gruyère), grated
2 oz (50 g) Parmesan cheese,
  grated

2 eggs, beaten,
pinch of salt
black pepper to taste

Combine the ingredients and mix well.

Vegetable and cheese fillings

Potato and cheese filling

2 medium potatoes
8 oz (225 g) hard cheese, grated
2 eggs, beaten

1 tablespoon butter
salt and black pepper to taste

Peel, boil and mash the potatoes. Combine them with the other ingredients and mix well.

Courgette and cheese filling

8 oz (225 g) courgettes or
 marrow
8 oz (225 g) cottage cheese, *or*
4 oz (100 g) cottage cheese plus
 4 oz (100 g) cream cheese

2 tablespoons chopped fresh
 mint or parsley
salt and black pepper to taste

Peel and coarsely grate the courgettes, drain them on absorbent paper and then mix them with the remaining ingredients.

Mushroom and cheese filling

8 oz (225 g) mushrooms,
 chopped
2 tablespoons vegetable oil
8 oz (225 g) Parmesan or other
 hard cheese, grated

2 eggs, beaten
salt and black pepper to taste

Lightly sauté the mushrooms in the oil and then mix them with the remaining ingredients.

Spinach and cheese filling

2 oz (50 g) butter or vegetable
 oil
1 medium onion, finely diced
1 lb (450 g) fresh spinach,
 washed and chopped, *or*
8 oz (225 g) frozen spinach,
 defrosted, drained, and finely
 chopped

2 oz (50 g) cream cheese or
 other soft cheese
1 egg, beaten
salt and black pepper to taste

Melt the butter in a heavy pan and sauté the onion until just soft. Add the chopped spinach, cover and cook over a low heat until wilted and tender. Allow to cool a little and then stir in the other ingredients.

Spinach and walnut filling

1 lb (450 g) fresh spinach, washed and finely chopped, *or*

8 oz (225 g) frozen spinach, defrosted, drained and finely chopped

2 tablespoons butter

2 oz (50 g) walnuts, finely chopped

2 oz (50 g) hard cheese, grated

1 egg, beaten

ground cinnamon, salt and pepper to taste

Melt the butter in a heavy pan and lightly sauté the walnuts. Add the spinach, cover and cook over a low heat until the spinach is wilted and tender. Allow to cool a little and then stir in the egg and cheese. Season to taste.

Vegetable and rice fillings

Use any of the fillings given for stuffed vegetables on pp. 104–11, or any of the pilav rice dishes (leftovers are fine) given on pp. 79–83 as fillings for savoury pastries.

Savoury shortcrust pastries

Shortcrust pastry dough

1 lb (450 g) plain flour

½ teaspoon salt

8 oz (225 g) margarine or butter

2 eggs, lightly beaten

a little water

Sift the flour and salt into a mixing bowl. Cut the margarine or butter into the bowl, and either rub it into the flour with your hands or use an electric beater. Add the eggs and mix them in with your fingers. Continue working the dough and slowly add enough water to form a soft ball that does not stick to the sides of the bowl. Cover the bowl with a damp cloth and set aside for 1 hour in a cool place. The dough is now ready to use.

Shortcrust yoghurt pastry dough

1 lb (450 g) plain flour
½ teaspoon salt
8 oz (225 g) margarine or butter

1 egg, beaten lightly
8 fl oz (225 ml) yoghurt

Follow the instructions for shortcrust pastry but use only the 1 egg and replace the water with yoghurt. If the final dough is a little too soft add more flour. Cover with a damp cloth and set aside in a cool place until ready for use.

Shortcrust circle pastries

Thinly roll out half the prepared shortcrust pastry dough, either the plain or yoghurt type, on a floured board. Cut out 2 in (5 cm) diameter circles and place them on an ungreased baking sheet. Put a full teaspoon of selected savoury filling on to each. Roll out the remaining pastry and cut into 2 in (5 cm) diameter circles. Place these on top of the filled circles and seal each well, using a little water or milk if needed. Pinch together and pattern the edges with a fork. Brush the tops with egg, beaten with a little water. Bake the pastries in a preheated oven at 350° F (175° C, gas mark 4) for about 40 minutes or until golden brown.

Shortcrust half-circle pastries

Roll out the prepared shortcrust pastry dough into a thin sheet or sheets. Cut out 3 in (7.5 cm) diameter circles. Put a teaspoon of selected savoury filling on each and then fold the dough over the filling to form a semi-circle. Seal the edges well together using a little milk or water if needed, and then pattern the join with your finger or a fork. Transfer the filled pastries to an ungreased baking tray. Brush the tops with egg beaten with a little water, and bake the pastries in a preheated oven at 350° F (175° C, gas mark 4) for about 40 minutes or until golden brown.

Shortcrust yoghurt pastry balls

Shortcrust yoghurt dough is the traditional dough for this pastry. Break off small, egg-size pieces and roll them into smooth balls.

Make a hole in each ball with your finger and force it open a little. Stuff the hole with one of the cheese fillings, leaving a little space at the top to seal up the hole again. Grease a baking tray and transfer the filled balls on to it. Brush them with egg beaten with a little water and bake them in a preheated oven at 400° F (205° C, gas mark 5) for 20 minutes or until golden brown. Serve hot.

Savoury fila pastries

Fila pastry dough is very versatile and most useful to the pastrycook. It is prepared in sheets of paper thinness which can be used singly or built up in layers to any thickness desired. The sheets are flexible and can be rolled or folded into a wide variety of shapes. Making *fila* pastry requires much skill and patience and it is difficult to make successfully at home. Fortunately it can be be bought ready-made in Greek grocery stores or delicatessens.

Ready-made *fila* dough is sold in standard-size packs of 1 lb (450 g) or 8 oz (225 g), containing about 24 or 12 sheets respectively. The normal size of a leaf of pastry is about 20 × 12 in (50 × 30 cm). Once a packet has been opened it should be used within a week, and the packet should always be tightly resealed after use since *fila* dries out and goes crumbly quickly in the air. It's a good idea to remove from the packet only as many sheets as you plan to use immediately. They keep flexible longer if immediately brushed with melted butter. Deep-frozen *fila* should be defrosted overnight in the refrigerator before use.

Fila triangle pastries

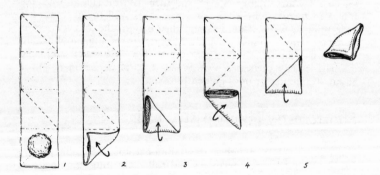

1   2   3   4   5

This is perhaps the most common *fila* pastry shape. Take 1 sheet of fila at a time and cut it into 4 pieces 6 × 10 in (15 × 25 cm). Brush each with melted butter, then fold in half lengthwise to give strips 3 × 10 in (7.5 × 25 cm). Brush each with melted butter again. Place a heaped teaspoon of selected savoury filling about 1 in (2.5 cm) from one end of a strip and fold the nearest corner over the filling to form a triangle. Fold the triangle over to form a two-layered triangle. Repeat all the way down the strip so that you end up with a many-layered triangle. Continue the procedure with more sheets of *fila* dough until all the filling is used up. Transfer the filled pastries to a greased baking tray and brush with butter once more. Bake in a preheated oven at 400° F (205° C, gas mark 5) for 35 to 40 minutes or until golden brown.

Fila square pastries

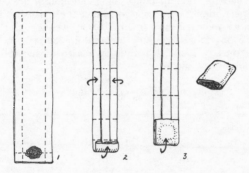

Prepare buttered strips 3 × 10 in (7.5 × 25 cm) as described for triangles. Place a heaped teaspoon of selected savoury filling about 1 in (2.5 cm) from the end of a strip. Fold over the long edges of the strip towards the middle to give a strip of about 2 in (5 cm) width. Now fold the short edge nearest the filling over it, and then fold again to form a 2 in (5 cm) square. Continue folding the square all the way down the strip so that you end up with a many-layered square. Repeat with the remaining filling and *fila* dough. Place the filled squares, seam side down, on a greased baking tray. Brush the squares with melted butter and bake them in a preheated oven at 400° F (205° C, gas mark 5) for 35 to 40 minutes or until golden brown.

Fila pastry rolls

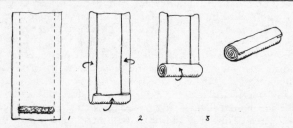

Brush a sheet of *fila* pastry dough with melted butter and cut it into four 5 × 12 in (12.5 × 30 cm) strips. Put 2 strips together one on top of another, to give you 2 double-layered strips. Place a full teaspoon or more of selected savoury filling on the short end of one of the strips and roll once. Now turn in the long edges a little to stop the filling spilling out, and then roll up the strip like a roll of carpet. Repeat for the remaining filling and dough. Place the filled rolls seam side down on a greased baking sheet. Brush them with melted butter and bake them in a preheated oven at 400° F (205° C, gas mark 5) for 35 to 40 minutes or until golden brown. Allow to cool, and then with a sharp knife slice each of the rolls on the diagonal into 2 or 3 pieces.

Fila pastry spirals

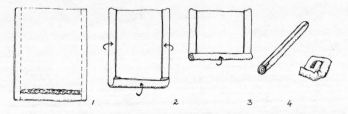

This is the traditional shape for spinach-filled pastries, although other fillings can be used. Brush a whole sheet of *fila* pastry with melted butter and spread some of the selected savoury filling along one of the short edges. Make the entire sheet into a long, thin roll. Curl this roll into a coil or spiral shape and transfer to a greased baking tray. Repeat for all the filling and pastry you have. Brush the coils with melted butter and bake in a preheated oven at 400° F (205° C, gas mark 5) for 35 to 40 minutes or until golden brown.

Fila tray pastries

Brush a large baking tray with melted butter. Cut 6 pieces of *fila* pastry dough to fit the tray and brush each with melted butter. Lay 3 pieces one on top of the other on the tray and spread over the top a selected savoury filling. Cover this with the 3 remaining pieces of dough and brush the top with melted butter. Bake in a preheated oven at 400° F (205° C, gas mark 5) for 35 to 40 minutes or until golden brown.

This method can also be used to make pies. Replace the baking tray with a 9 in (22.5 cm) pie dish. Mould 3 sheets of *fila* pastry into the fish to form a shell for the bottom and sides of the dish. Put in the selected filling. Cover the dish with another 3 sheets of *fila* dough and seal the top and bottom edges together with melted butter. Tidy up the edges by folding over or cutting off the over-hang. Bake the pie(s) in a preheated oven at 400° F (205° C, gas mark 5) for 35 to 40 minutes or until golden brown.

Deep fried fila pastries

These are a Tunisian variation of *fila* pastries, called *brik*. The various filled pastries are prepared in the same ways as described above, but instead of being baked they are deep fried in moderately hot oil until nicely browned then drained on absorbent paper before serving. Triangular or square *brik* pastries are the most common.

Savoury flaky pastries

Shop-bought flaky pastry dough is perfectly satisfactory and will make good filled pastries. The dough recipe given here is for those people who want the extra satisfaction of making the pastry themselves.

Flaky pastry dough

1 lb (450 g) plain flour
1 teaspoon salt
4 tablespoons olive oil or other vegetable oil

juice of 1 lemon
about 16 fl oz (450 ml) iced water
8 oz (225 g) margarine

Sift the flour and salt into a large bowl and add the oil and lemon juice. Knead in enough iced water to form a soft dough. Roll the dough on a floured board into a rectangle about 2 × 8 in (5 × 20 cm). Spread the margarine over the top, fold the pastry into 3 and then place it in the refrigerator for 30 minutes. Remove it and roll the dough into the same size rectangular shape as before, but this time roll across the dough at right-angles to the first direction of rolling. Fold into 3 again and refrigerate for 30 minutes. Repeat twice more, changing the rolling direction each time. After the final 30 minutes' refrigeration the pastry is ready for use.

Preparing savoury flaky pastries

Roll out the prepared flaky pastry dough as thinly as possible. Cut it into 4 in (10 cm) squares and/or 4 in (10 cm) diameter circles, and put a full teaspoon of selected savoury filling in the centre of each. Fold the squares into triangles and the circles into half-circles, and press or pinch the edges together to seal them. Put the filled pastries on an ungreased baking tray and brush them with egg mixed with a little water. Bake them in a preheated oven at 375° F (190° C, gas mark 5) for 30 minutes or until golden brown. Sometimes the baked pastries are sprinkled with sesame seeds before being put in the oven. Alternatively, deep fry the pastries in hot oil and then drain them on absorbent paper.

Sumboosak pastries

Sumboosak are small, half-moon-shaped pastries. They are made from a dough that is traditionally prepared from equal quantities of water, oil and butter, with enough flour added to form a soft dough. This particular recipe is Lebanese.

Sumboosak pastry dough

approximately 1 lb (450 g) plain flour
1 teaspoon salt

4 oz (100 g) butter, melted
4 fl oz (100 ml) vegetable oil
4 fl oz (100 ml) hot water

Sift the flour and salt together. Put the butter, oil and hot water in a large mixing bowl and vigorously whisk together – alternatively use an electric blender. Slowly stir the flour into the mixture, working the dough with your hands until you form a smooth, soft dough that does not stick to the sides of the bowl.

Preparing savoury sumboosak pastries

Pinch off small, egg-size pieces of the prepared dough, roll them into balls in the palms of your hands and then roll each out thinly into a circle shape. Place a full teaspoon of one of the spinach or cheese fillings in the centre of each circle and fold one side of each circle over to form half-circles. Press or pinch the edge with a fork or your finger to seal them. Transfer the *sumboosak* to a lightly greased baking tray. Bake them in a preheated oven at 400° F (205° C, gas mark 6) for 5 minutes, then reduce the heat to 350° F (175° C, gas mark 4) and bake for a further 30 minutes or until they are lightly browned. Sometimes the *sumboosak* are brushed with beaten egg and sprinkled with sesame seeds before baking. They can also be deep fried in hot oil. If you cook them by this method drain them on absorbent paper before serving.

Sweet pastries

'The faithful are sweet, the wicked sour.'

The Prophet Mohammed

Baklava and *kadayif (konafa)*, the first 2 types of pastry to be dealt with in this section, are very popular all over the Middle East and are served with coffee or tea at any time of the day. Both pastries, which will be familiar to anyone who has eaten in Greek or Turkish restaurants, are prepared and baked in large, shallow, square or round tins and then covered in a sweep syrup. Baklava are made from *fila* pastry dough with a nut filling, and sometimes, but more rarely, a cheese or fruit filling. *Kadayif* is made from a flour and water dough shaped into long, vermicelli-like straws which when baked look like Shredded Wheat. It is not easily available in the West, although some Greek shops stock it. Shredded Wheat can be used as a substitute. The usual filling is again a nut mixture, but more rarely a sweet, creamy cheese spread is used.

Both baklava and *kadayif* can be made in larger quantities than needed and stored in the deep freeze or refrigerator.

Baklava

The recipe is given in 3 parts. First come 4 different types of filling. Then follows the method for making the syrup, which is poured over the baklava after baking. Finally I describe the way baklava is put together from the *fila* pastry dough, the filling and the syrup. I suggest that you buy ready-made dough.

All the recipes make sufficient filling for 1 lb (450 g) *fila* dough. The first 2 fillings are the ones most commonly used.

Chopped nut and cinnamon filling

1 lb (450 g) nuts, such as walnuts, chopped; almonds, blanched and coarsely ground; pistachio nuts, chopped; hazelnuts, chopped; or, as a last resort, peanuts, chopped. Alternatively a mixture of nuts may be used	2 oz (50 g) sugar 2 teaspoons ground cinnamon

Combine the ingredients and mix well.

Chopped nut and sesame filling

12 oz (350 g) nuts, chopped (see recipe above) 4 oz (100 g) sesame seeds, browned in 2 tablespoons butter	2 oz (50 g) sugar peel of 1 lemon, grated

Combine the ingredients and mix well

Sweet cheese filling

1 lb (450 g) ricotta cheese   Cinnamon and sugar to taste

Beat the cheese, cinnamon and sugar into a smooth filling.

Apple filling

2 apples, cored and finely diced   1 teaspoon ground cinnamon
2 oz (50 g) chopped nuts (see   2 oz (50 g) sugar
   first filling recipe)   juice of 1 lemon

Combine the ingredients and mix well.

Syrup for baklava

12 oz (350 g) sugar (up to 1 lb/   juice of 1 lemon
   450 g sugar may be used for   1 tablespoon orange blossom
   sweeter syrups)   water or rosewater if
8 fl oz (225 ml) water   available

Dissolve the sugar in the water and lemon juice in a pan. Bring the mixture to the boil and simmer for 10 to 15 minutes or until slightly viscous. Stir in the orange blossom water or rosewater and remove from the heat.

The syrup should be cooled or even slightly chilled, and then poured over the hot pastries as soon as they come out of the oven.

Making the baklava

Recipe 1

1 lb (450 g) *fila* pastry dough   selected filling (see above)
8 oz (225 g) unsalted butter,   syrup (see above)
   melted

Choose a large, not too deep, baking tin or dish (e.g. 12 x 16 in/30 x 40 cm). Brush half the pastry sheets and the baking tin sides and bottom with melted butter. Fit the sheets into the bottom of the tin one at a time, folding to fit as necessary. Spread the prepared filling over the top in a ½ to ¾ in (1.3 to 1.8 cm) layer. Brush the remaining sheets of pastry with melted butter and place them one at a time on top of the filling. Again fold to fit as necessary. If there is any butter left pour it over the top layer. With a very sharp knife cut through all the layers diagonally to form diamond shapes.

Bake in a preheated oven at 375° F (190° C, gas mark 5) for 30 minutes and then at 450° F (230° C, gas mark 7) for 15 minutes. The baklava should be nicely browned. Remove from the oven and immediately pour over the cold or chilled syrup. Allow to cool before serving.

Alternatively, for very moist baklava, pour two-thirds of the syrup over the hot baklava, allow to cool and then pour over the remaining syrup.

Some people prefer to omit the syrup and serve the baklava crisp and sprinkled with a little icing sugar.

Recipe 2

Take 2 or 3 sheets of *fila* pastry dough and brush them with melted butter. Lay one sheet on top of the other and place 4 or 5 tablespoons of selected filling along the long side of the top sheet. Roll it all up like a piece of carpet and place the roll in a buttered dish. Cut the roll to fit the dish if necessary. Repeat until all the *fila* dough and filling has been used up and pack the rolls close together in the dish. Brush them with melted butter and then cut them diagonally into 2 to 3 in (5 to 7.5 cm) lengths. Bake the baklava at 350° F (175° C, gas mark 4) until nicely browned. Remove them from the oven and pour cold syrup over them. Allow the baklava to cool before serving.

Puff pastry baklava

To make a quick baklava replace the *fila* pastry with 1 lb (450 g) puff pastry. Divide the pastry into 4 equal portions, and roll each portion into a sheet the size of the baking tin. Arrange 2 sheets below the filling and 2 sheets above. Otherwise follow the same method as for ordinary baklava. Baking times may have to be cut slightly.

Kadayif

Kadayif dough is made by pouring and shaking a flour and water batter through a sieve on to a hot metal plate. The dough forms in long, white strands which are scraped off the heat while still soft. These soft, vermicelli-shaped strands are layered on the base of a baking tin, buttered and spread with a filling, which is then covered with another layer of the buttered dough. The whole thing is baked, and finally coated, while still hot, in cold syrup. If *kadayif* dough is unavailable, slightly crushed Shredded Wheat can also be used to make separate small *kadayif* pastries, which, if you were using ordinary *kadayif* dough, would normally require a lot of expertise to prepare.

Each of the following 2 recipes makes enough filling for 1 lb (450g) *kadayif* dough or about 12 large Shredded Wheat.

Chopped nut and cinnamon filling

10 oz (275 g) walnuts or pistachios, chopped; alternatively other nuts or a combination of nuts may be used	2 tablespoons sugar 2 teaspoons ground cinnamon

Combine the ingredients and mix together.

Sweet cheese filling

1 lb (450 g) ricotta cheese
ground cinnamon and sugar to
    taste

Beat the cheese and cinnamon and sugar to taste into a smooth filling.

Syrup for kadayif

Use the same syrup recipe as given for baklava on p. 141.

Making the kadayif

1 lb (450 g) *kadayif* dough, *or* 12 Shredded Wheat	selected filling syrup

Remove any lumps from the *kadayif* dough by gently separating the strands with your fingers. Place half the dough in a buttered, not too deep, large square or round baking dish (e.g. 12 x 16 in/30 x 40 cm) and brush with butter. Alternatively if using Shredded Wheat, break up half the Shredded Wheat and lay the shreds in the buttered dish and brush with butter. Now evenly spread the filling over the dough or Shredded Wheat, cover evenly with the remaining dough or Shredded Wheat and brush generously with butter. Bake the *kadayif* in a preheated oven at 375° F (190° C, gas mark 4) for 45 minutes or until golden. Remove it from the oven and pour over the cold syrup. Cool and cut the *kadayif* into small squares.

Individual kadayif

Using a sharp knife hollow out the centre of Shredded Wheat biscuits and stuff with a selected filling. Brush generously with melted butter. Bake the filled Shredded Wheat in a preheated oven at 375° F (190° C, gas mark 4) for 30 minutes and then pour cold syrup over them.

Fruit kadayif

Follow the recipe given above for making *kadayif*, but replace the nut or cheese fillings with layers of sliced bananas or peaches.

Maamoul

Maamoul are small, round pastries stuffed with a nut or date filling. They will keep for weeks in an airtight tin. Two types of pastry are used – one flour-based and the other semolina-based. The semolina pastry takes longer to make but the *maamoul* made from it are especially good. Recipes for both doughs and 2 fillings are given, together with the method of preparation. Follow whichever combination of filling and dough you like.

Nut filling

10 oz (275 g) walnuts, finely chopped
6 oz (175 g) sugar

1 tablespoon ground cinnamon

Combine the ingredients and mix well. If walnuts are not available almonds or pistachios can be used.

Date filling

1 lb (450 g) dates, stoned and chopped
2 tablespoons butter

2 oz (50 g) walnuts, finely chopped (optional)

Put the dates and butter in a saucepan and stir over a low heat until the dates have softened and become pasty. Stir in the nuts and cool.

Flour dough

8 oz (225 g) butter   1 lb (450 g) plain flour
2 tablespoons sugar   3 tablespoons milk

Cream the butter and sugar. Sift the flour into a large bowl and work the butter and sugar into it by hand until well blended. Gradually add milk to form a soft dough.

Semolina dough

8 oz (225 g) butter, melted   approximately 4 fl oz (100 ml)
1 lb (225 g) semolina   warm milk
2 tablespoons flour

Thoroughly mix the melted butter and semolina. Cover and leave the mixture overnight. Add the flour and then slowly add the warm milk. Knead the mixture into a smooth dough, adding more milk if necessary.

Preparing the maamoul

Pinch off a walnut-size ball of whichever dough you have made and place it in the palm of your hand. Using your forefinger push a hole into the centre and expand it a little. Support the outside shell with the palm of your hand. Fill the hole with the nut or date filling, leaving enough space at the top to fold over the hole and fill it up. Press the filled dough ball on to a lightly greased baking sheet and decorate the top with the tines of a fork. Repeat for the remaining dough and filling.

Bake the *maamoul* at 350° F (175° C, gas mark 4) for 15 to 20 minutes. The bottoms of the *maamoul* should be lightly browned but the tops should stay pale and, while still hot, look slightly uncooked. Leave them to cool and then sift icing sugar over them. Store the *maamoul* in an airtight tin.

PUDDINGS, CAKES, SWEETMEATS AND BISCUITS

The Prophet Mohammed, said to have had a sweet tooth, is reported to have once said: 'The love of sweetmeats comes from the Faith.' Perhaps this is why sweet things are so popular in the Middle East, and the region's great tradition of hospitality inevitably involves the serving of sweetmeats. Deep fried cakes, biscuits, rice and semolina puddings, halva and Turkish delight are all great favourites. Sweet pastries are also popular, and recipes for them can be found in the previous chapter.

Rice pudding

Rice pudding is popular as a dessert and as a breakfast dish. It is normally served chilled, sprinkled with cinnamon or ginger.

8 fl oz (225 ml) water
1¼ pt (725 ml) milk
3 tablespoons sugar
4 oz (100 g) rice

1 tablespoon rosewater or
   orange blossom water
   (optional)
pinch of salt
ground cinnamon

Put the water, milk and sugar in a heavy pan and bring to the boil. Add the rice, reduce the heat, cover and simmer for 25 minutes. Add the rosewater and a pinch of salt, stir and simmer a further 5 minutes. Pour the pudding into serving bowls and chill. Serve them topped with cinnamon and, if you wish, some chopped walnuts or blanched chopped almonds or even dessicated coconut.

Damascus semolina pudding

This pudding is a popular breakfast dish in Syria. It also makes a lovely dessert.

1 pt (575 ml) water
8 oz (225 g) sugar
juice of ½ lemon
6 oz (175 g) semolina

4 oz (100 g) butter or margarine
2 oz (50 g) blanched almonds
ground cinnamon

Combine the water, sugar and lemon juice and bring the mixture to the boil. Simmer it for 10 minutes. Melt the butter in a heavy pan, lightly sauté the almonds and add the semolina. Cook, stirring, over a moderate heat until the semolina is lightly browned. Stir into this the sugar and water mixture and then leave the pudding to cook for a further 2 to 3 minutes. Remove the pan from the heat and serve the pudding hot or cooled with cinnamon sprinkled over and, if you wish, a dollop of thick cream. (Orange juice may be substituted for half the water.)

Sweet couscous

8 oz (225 g) couscous
10 fl oz (275 ml) hot water
2 oz (50 g) butter, melted
12 dates, stoned
12 almonds
4 oz (225 g) mixed nuts, finely
  chopped

2 oz (50 g) currants
4 oz (100 g) sugar
juice of 1 orange
1 oz (25 g) icing sugar
2 teaspoons ground cinnamon

Put the couscous in a bowl and stir in the hot water. Set aside for 10 minutes. Stuff each of the dates with an almond. Put the couscous in a colander or sieve over a pan of boiling water and steam it for 15 minutes. Rub the melted butter into the couscous and then steam it for a further 15 minutes.

Combine the nuts, currants, sugar and orange juice and fold the mixture into the couscous. Pile it on to a serving dish in a mound and decorate the top with almond-stuffed dates. Sprinkle with icing sugar and cinnamon before serving.

Turkish delight (locum)

Making traditional Turkish delight is difficult and time-consuming, and in any case many of the recipes are kept a closely guarded secret by the Turkish confectioners whose families have followed a particular recipe for centuries. The simplified recipe given here is perhaps not as good as that served to the ladies of a Sultan's harem, but certainly better than the commercial Turkish delight now sold.

12 fl oz (350 ml) water
4 fl oz (100 ml) orange juice
juice of 1 lemon
¼ oz (6 g) gelatine
1 lb (450 g) sugar
a few drops of cochineal or
  other food colouring
  (optional)

2 oz (50 g) pistachios or
  almonds, chopped
icing sugar for dusting

In a heavy saucepan combine the water and orange and lemon juices. Sprinkle over the gelatine and stir. Slowly heat the pan, stirring, until all the gelatine is dissolved. Increase the heat and stir in the sugar and cochineal. Bring to a slow boil and simmer for 20 minutes, stirring now and again. Add the chopped nuts. Remove from the heat and cool, stirring, until it reaches blood heat. Pour the mixture into a square or rectangular tin, and set the tin in a dish of cold water. Cover the tin with a cloth and leave it in the refrigerator until the Turkish delight has set. Cut into squares with an oiled knife and dust with icing sugar. Store in an airtight container.

Sweet grain and bean pudding

This unusual but delicious sweet is an old Turkish dish originally designed to use up leftovers. You should therefore use the recipe only as a guide.

2 oz (50 g) haricot beans,
  soaked overnight and drained
2 oz (50 g) chick peas, soaked
  overnight and drained
2 oz (50 g) rice, washed and
  drained
2 oz (50 g) wholewheat or
  bulgar wheat

2 oz (50 g) currants
2 oz (50 g) dried apricots, dates
  or figs, chopped
4 oz (100 g) almonds, blanched
4 oz (100 g) sugar
walnuts and sultanas for
  garnishing

Cook the beans and peas in separate pots until just tender but not very soft. Drain and discard the liquid. Set the beans and chick peas on one side to cool. Cook the rice and wholewheat in separate pots, or if using bulgar wheat cook it and the rice together, until both grains are very tender. Drain, and reserve any liquid. Combine the beans, chick peas, hot rice and wheat, mix well and stir in the currants, dried apricots, almonds and sugar. Add enough of the reserved cooking liquid from the rice and wheat to moisten the mixture and then chill it. Serve the pudding in individual bowls decorated with walnuts, sultanas and, if you wish, a tablespoon of fresh whipped cream.

Fried dough balls in syrup

Awwaymet in the Lebanon, or *zalabia* as they are called in Egypt, are small balls of yeasted dough, fried in oil and then soaked in syrup. Serve them hot and golden brown, piled high on a serving dish and sprinkled with sugar and cinnamon.

½ oz (12 g) fresh yeast, *or*
¼ oz (6 g) dried yeast
1 teaspoon sugar
1 lb (450 g) plain flour
16 fl oz (450 ml) warm water

½ teaspoon salt
sweet syrup (see p. 141) or
    honey
oil for shallow frying

Dissolve the yeast and sugar in a little of the water and leave the mixture in a warm place to froth up before stirring in the remaining water. Combine the flour and salt, slowly stir in the yeast mixture and beat into a smooth dough. Set the dough aside in a warm place covered with a damp cloth and leave it to rise for 2 to 3 hours. Before use the dough should be well fermented and sponge-like.

Heat about 2 in (5 cm) of oil in a saucepan over a moderate heat. Using a wet teaspoon, scoop up small balls of dough and drop them into the oil. Fry a few at a time until they are golden brown. Turn them over once or twice during frying. Drain the *awwaymet* on absorbent paper and dip them while still hot into a bowl of syrup or honey. Remove and serve them sprinkled with sugar and cinnamon.

For moulding perfect balls or designing other shapes of *awwaymet* the dough can be forced out of a pastry bag. Sometimes the dough is divided up and each portion dyed a different colour with food colouring. If 2 or more colours are used you can make rosettes of dough in the hot oil.

Dimple cakes

These round, syrupy cakes with a dimple in the middle are also aptly called ladies' navels.

4 oz (100 g) butter, slightly
    softened
4 oz (100 g) sugar
4 eggs

1 lb (450 g) plain flour
a little milk
sweet syrup (see page 141)
whipped cream

Beat the butter and sugar together until light and fluffy. Beat in the eggs and then slowly stir in the flour. Add a little milk if the dough is too stiff, but note that you are aiming for a firm, not soft, dough.

Pinch off pieces of dough the size of a small egg and form them into balls. Push a dimple into the centre of each ball, using the knuckles of 2 fingers together. Place them on an ungreased baking tray and bake in a preheated oven at 350° F (175° C, gas mark 4) for 20 to 25 minutes or until nicely browned. While still hot, pour syrup over the cakes and leave them to cool. Place a knob of cream in each dimple and serve.

The cakes can also be cooked by gentle frying in melted butter. If cooked in this way make slightly smaller cakes than described above.

Yoghurt fritters

This is a Turkish treat – unusual, but quick and easy to make.

1 pt (575 ml) yoghurt	peel of 1 lemon, grated
2 eggs	oil for deep frying
8 oz (225 g) flour	caster sugar

Put the eggs and yoghurt into a bowl and beat well together. Stir in the lemon peel and then gradually add the flour, beating all the time. Heat the oil until it is just starting to smoke and then drop in teaspoons of batter. Deep fry the fritters golden brown. Drain them on absorbent paper and then roll them in caster sugar. For an extra treat serve the fritters with a blob of thick cream.

Palace bread

This recipe is so called because there's almost no bread in it, but rather a lot of sugar, honey and butter.

8 oz (225 g) honey	4 oz (100 g) breadcrumbs, or
8 oz (225 g) butter	more as needed
8 oz (225 g) sugar	

Put the honey, butter and sugar into a saucepan and heat, stirring, until melted and well mixed. Stir in the breadcrumbs and cook the mixture over a gentle heat, stirring, for 10 minutes or until a sticky mass is formed. Add more breadcrumbs if necessary. Pour the mixture into a shallow tin or mould and cool. Cut into squares. Serve with whipped fresh cream or sour cream.

Little semolina cakes

These are very rich and sweet little cakes, only for special occasions.

8 oz (225 g) semolina
8 fl oz (225 g) olive oil
4 oz (100 g) clear honey
2 oz (50 g) icing sugar
juice of 1 small orange
2 teaspoons grated orange peel
½ teaspoon ground cinnamon
¼ teaspoon ground cloves
1 teaspoon baking powder

Syrup
8 oz (225 g) sugar
5 fl oz (150 ml) water
chopped walnuts or almonds
    for garnishing

Stir the semolina into the olive oil to form a smooth paste. Stir in the remaining ingredients (but not those for the syrup) and mix well. The dough should just hold its shape. Add more semolina if it doesn't. Preheat the oven to 350° F (175° C, gas mark 4). Pinch off large walnut-size lumps of dough, roll them in your hands and slightly flatten the tops and bottoms. Place the cakes on a greased baking sheet, pattern the tops with a fork and bake them in the preheated oven for 20 minutes.

To make the syrup, bring the sugar and water to the boil and simmer for 10 minutes or until the syrup has thickened. Arrange the cakes on a serving dish, pour over them the hot syrup and sprinkle with chopped nuts. Alternatively allow the cakes to cool a little, dip them into the hot syrup and arrange them in little individual paper cups.

Date cakes

1 lb (450 g) pitted dates, finely
    chopped
4 oz (100 g) walnuts, chopped
4 oz (100 g) butter, melted

approximately 6 oz (175 g)
    plain flour
double cream for garnishing

In a large bowl combine the dates, walnuts and half the butter. Mix well, and work in by hand enough flour to form a stiff mixture. Form the mixture into flat cakes about 2 in (5 cm) in diameter. Fry the cakes in the remaining butter until nicely browned on both sides. Serve hot with a blob of cream.

Turkish apple cake

This cake is delicious, and since it contains no fat it is a treat slimmers can enjoy.

1½ lb (675 g) cooking apples, peeled, cored and chopped	4 oz (100 g) plain flour
juice of 1 lemon	pinch of salt
2 oz (50 g) mixed nuts	1 teaspoon baking powder
2 oz (50 g) sultanas	½ teaspoon vanilla essence
4 oz (100 g) sugar	1 egg, beaten

Preheat the oven to 350° F (175° C, gas mark 4). Put the chopped apple into a large bowl and sprinkle it with the lemon juice. Combine the nuts, sultanas, sugar, flour, salt and baking powder and mix well. Stir the mixture into the apple. Stir in the vanilla essence and beaten egg and mix well. Pour the mixture into a lightly oiled cake tin and bake in the preheated oven for 20 minutes, or until lightly browned on top. Serve hot or cold with cream. For a moister cake, add to the ingredients a little fruit juice, cider or water.

Variation
This basic recipe can be adapted successfully for other fruits. Pears and plums together make a good combination.

Almond biscuits (cookies)

10 oz (275 g) butter, slightly softened	2 tablespoons milk
6 oz (175 g) caster sugar	1 teaspoon almond essence
1 lb (450 g) plain flour	approximately 2 oz (50 g) blanched almonds
1 egg, lightly beaten	

Cream the butter and sugar together until light and fluffy. Gradually add the flour, mixing all the time, and then the egg, milk and almond essence. The resultant dough should be soft and slightly crumbly. Pinch off walnut-size pieces of dough and roll them into smooth balls with slightly flattened tops. Press a blanched almond into the top of each and place the biscuits on an ungreased baking sheet. Bake them in a preheated oven at 350° F (175° C, gas mark 4) for 12 to 15 minutes. The biscuits should remain unbrowned. Cool and store them in an airtight tin.

Nut moon biscuits

6 oz (175 g) butter, slightly
  softened
2 oz (50 g) caster sugar
12 oz (350 g) plain flour
approximately 3 fl oz (75 ml)
  milk
8 oz (225 g) walnuts, ground or
  finely chopped

3 oz (75 g) sugar
½ tablespoon rosewater or
  orange blossom water, if
  available
icing sugar

Beat the butter and sugar until creamy, light and fluffy. Gradually
fold in the flour and enough milk to form a softish dough. Knead
the dough for a few minutes. Combine the walnuts, sugar and rose
water or orange blossom water and mix well. Roll the dough into
a sheet ¼ in (6 mm) thick and cut out 2 to 3 in (5 to 7.5 cm) circles.
Place a heaped teaspoon of the nut and sugar filling on to each and
then fold them over to form half moons. Press the edges together
to seal in the filling and decorate the tops of the biscuits with the
tines of a fork. Lay the biscuits on an ungreased baking sheet and
bake them in a preheated oven at 350° F (175° C, gas mark 4) for 20
to 25 minutes, or until lightly browned. Cool, and sift icing sugar
over them. Store in an airtight tin.

Persian button biscuits

8 oz (225 g) butter, slightly
  softened
8 oz (225 g) caster sugar
2 egg yolks

8 oz (225 g) plain flour
1 teaspoon baking powder
1 teaspoon vanilla essence
1 teaspoon almond essence

Beat the butter and sugar together until light and fluffy. Add the
egg yolks, vanilla and almond essences and mix well. Sift the flour
and baking powder together and gradually fold into the butter mixture. Beat or knead into a smooth, well-mixed dough. Pinch off
smaller than walnut-size pieces of dough and form them into
smooth, round balls with slightly flattened tops. Place the biscuits
on an ungreased baking sheet and bake them in a preheated oven at
250° F (120° C, gas mark 1) for 20 minutes. Cool, and store them
in an airtight tin.

Spiced yeasted biscuits

½ oz (12 g) fresh yeast, *or*
¼ oz (6 g) dried yeast
2 fl oz (50 ml) warm water
1 lb (450 g) plain flour
10 oz (275 g) sugar

½ teaspoon salt
½ teaspoon ground cloves
½ teaspoon allspice
6 oz (175 g) butter
1 egg, beaten

Dissolve the yeast in the warm water, add a little of the sugar, mix well and set the mixture aside in a warm place to froth up. Mix together the dry ingredients and rub in the butter. Add the yeast mixture and knead, adding more water if needed, to form a soft dough. Knead for a further 5 minutes, cover, and set aside in a warm place for 1 hour. Roll the dough into a sheet about ¼ in (6 mm) thick and cut out 3 in (7.5 cm) diameter circles. Press a design around the edges and in the middle of each circle, using your finger or a fork, and place them on an ungreased baking sheet. Cover them with a damp cloth and leave them to rise in a warm place for 30 minutes. Brush the biscuits with beaten egg and bake them in a preheated oven at 350° F (175° C, gas mark 4) for 30 minutes or until nicely browned. Cool, and store them in an airtight tin.

Lebanese doughnuts

2 eggs, beaten until fluffy
8 oz (225 g) caster sugar
2 tablespoons yoghurt
peel of 1 lemon, grated

12 oz (350 g) plain flour
2 oz (50 g) margarine or butter,
  softened
1 teaspoon baking powder

Preheat the oven to 350° F (175° C, gas mark 4). Using an electric mixer if possible, beat the eggs, margarine, sugar and yoghurt together until the sugar loses its texture. Mix in the lemon peel. Sift together the flour and baking powder and gradually fold into the egg mixture. Mix into a smooth, firm dough. Add more flour if necessary. Pinch off large walnut-size lumps of dough and roll into 6 in (15 cm) long ropes. Overlap the ends and press together. Place them on a lightly greased baking sheet and bake until golden brown (about 20 minutes).

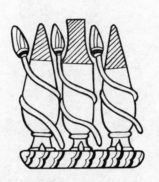

FRUIT DISHES

To follow a large Middle Eastern meal with a pudding or very sweet pastry would be too much for the system, and fruit is the usual dessert. During the summer months in particular fruits are abundant and varied, and figs, peaches, apricots, quinces, oranges, melons, apples, black cherries, grapes and dates are just some of those available. They are served plain and sometimes, if you are lucky, peeled by your host or hostess. Sliced or grated fruit, perfumed with rosewater or orange blossom water and mixed with crushed ice, is also popular. In winter months dried fruit compôtes and hot desserts such as stuffed apples are prepared.

Fresh fruit compôte

The combination of fruit given in this recipe is only a suggestion, and you may substitute any mixture of fruits or a single fruit.

4 oz (100 g) sugar
16 fl oz (450 ml) water
2 peaches
2 tart apples, washed
8 oz (225 g) plums, washed, stoned and halved

8 oz (225 g) strawberries, washed
2 sticks cinnamon, *or*
1 teaspoon ground cinnamon
juice of 1 lemon

Put the sugar and water in a pan and bring to the boil. Set to simmer. Plunge the peaches in a pan of boiling water and then immediately remove them and drop them into cold water. The skins will now come off easily. Slice the skinned peaches and the apples and put them into the simmering syrup. Add the plums, strawberries, cinnamon and lemon juice. Simmer for 15 minutes, stirring occasionally. Remove cinnamon sticks (if used). Leave to cool, chill, and serve with whipped cream.

Variations
If rosewater is available add 1 or 2 drops to the simmering fruit. Try cardamom in place of the cinnamon for a different flavour.

Dried fruit compôte

1 lb (450 g) dried fruit(s) (e.g. apricots, apples, prunes, figs etc.)
2 oz (50 g) sugar

juice of 1 lemon
chopped nuts and double cream for garnishing

Cover the dried fruit with water and leave to soak overnight. Put the fruit and liquid into a pan and add the sugar. Bring to the boil, reduce the heat and simmer until the fruit is very soft. Add the lemon juice and stir. Serve hot or cold with cream and sprinkled with chopped nuts.

Apple, banana and lemon dessert

8 oz (225 g) sugar
8 fl oz (225 ml) water
4 tart apples, peeled, cored and sliced

2 bananas, peeled and sliced
peel of 2 lemons, grated
juice of 2 lemons
2 teaspoons ground cinnamon

Put the sugar and water in a heavy pan and bring to the boil. Add the apples, bananas, lemon peel, lemon juice and cinnamon. Simmer until nearly all the liquid has evaporated and the mixture is thick. Cool and serve. Cream or yoghurt garnished with toasted almonds go well with this dish.

Uncooked stuffed apples

4 sweet, firm apples, cored
juice of 1 lemon
3 oz (50 g) whole dates
1 oz (25 g) raisins
4 fl oz (100 ml) yoghurt

1 tablespoon sugar
¼ teaspoon ground cardamom
¼ teaspoon ground cinnamon
2 oz (50 g) almonds, lightly roasted

Put the apples in a bowl, cover in water, stir in the lemon juice and set aside. Stone the dates, set 4 aside and finely chop the rest. Add the raisins, yoghurt, sugar, cardamom and cinnamon to the chopped dates and mix well. Stuff each of the reserved whole dates with an almond and crush the remaining almonds.

Drain the apples and stuff with the yoghurt mixture. Top each one with an almond-stuffed date and sprinkle with crushed almonds. Chill and serve.

Israeli fruit salad

Serves 6

1 medium ripe avocado, peeled, stoned and chopped
1 orange, peeled and separated into segments
4 oz (100 g) mild cheese, cut into small cubes
juice of 1 lemon
1 tablespoon sugar
1 tablespoon chopped walnuts
pinch of ground cardamom or cinnamon
1 small lettuce

Combine the avocado, orange and cheese and mix well. Sprinkle with lemon juice, sugar, walnuts and spice. Chill, and serve on a bed of lettuce leaves.

Sweet preserved pears

The recipe for this popular Syrian sweet is for 4 lb (2 kg) of pears, but if you wish to experiment with a smaller amount use 1 lb (450 g) and reduce the other ingredients accordingly.

4 lb (2 kg) pears, peeled and quartered
1 lb (450 g) sugar
3 in (7.5 cm) piece of ginger root, peeled
2 teaspoons ground cardamom
2 sticks cinnamon
peel of 3 lemons, grated

Combine all the ingredients except the lemon peel, just cover with water and leave overnight. Bring the mixture to the boil, add the lemon peel and set to simmer. Skim off any scum that forms and leave to simmer until the liquid gets thick and syrupy. Remove from the heat. Cool, remove the cinnamon sticks and ginger root, and pack the pears and syrup into preserving jars. Seal tightly and they will be good for at least a month.

BEVERAGES

Turkish coffee (kahve)

Turkish coffee is served throughout the Middle East, and although it may have originated in Turkey the name now implies only a particular method of preparation.

Freshly roasted coffee beans are ground to a fine powder which is then boiled with sugar and a small amount of water. The coffee is served very strong in small cups, usually accompanied by a glass of cold water. As soon as the grains settle in the cup the coffee is sipped with alternate sips of water. The coffee is normally brewed one cup at a time, and each person will be asked how much sugar he or she wants in their cup. In a restaurant or café the coffee is served in three ways, very sweet (*sekerli*) sweet (*orta*) or unsweetened (*sade*).

Method per person

Put 2 teaspoons of very finely ground coffee in a small pot or Turkish coffee pot with as much sugar as you wish (usually 1 to 2 teaspoons). Add a half cup of boiling water and bring the pot to the boil. Immediately remove it from the heat and allow to cool a little. Bring to the boil again, and again immediately remove from the heat. For very strong coffee repeat this process once more. Pour the coffee into a small cup and allow the grains to settle before drinking. Stroking the froth with the back of a spoon helps the settling process.

The coffee can be served with cream, and sometimes a pod of cardamom is added to the cup.

Moroccan tea

Tea was introduced into Morocco by the British in the nineteenth century, and it is now as popular and as much of a tradition there as in Britain. Moroccan tea is prepared with green China tea, mint leaves and sugar, and served very hot in narrow glasses. (If you are using glasses, make sure you have the kind that will withstand very hot liquids.) In hot weather the tea is drained from the leaves, chilled and served cold.

Method for 4 people

Put 3 teaspoons of green tea in a warmed teapot, add 2 tablespoons of sugar (add more or less if you wish) and a handful of fresh mint leaves. Push the leaves to the bottom of the pot. Pour over enough boiling water for 4 people and allow the tea to steep for 3 or 4 minutes. Stir, allow to settle, and then pour the tea into serving glasses.

Orange blossom water, if available, or a little grated orange peel added to the pot before the boiling water is poured in, gives the tea a special fragrance.

Spice tea

2 in (5 cm) piece of ginger root,
  peeled
2 whole cloves
2 cinnamon sticks
1 tablespoon anise seeds

or

1 tablespoon ground cinnamon
1 tablespoon caraway seeds
1 tablespoon anise seeds
pinch of nutmeg

plus for either set of ingredients

boiling water for 4 people
4 whole almonds or walnuts

Put all the ingredients except the nuts in a pan, and gently boil for about 5 minutes or until the water darkens. Put a nut in each person's cup, pour the spice tea over it and serve with sugar.

Cinnamon tea

Boil for 5 minutes 2 or 3 cinnamon sticks with enough water to make tea for 4 to 6 people. Put ordinary tea or tea bags into the teapot and then pour in the boiling cinnamon water. Leave the tea to brew for 2 minutes and then pour. Sometimes this tea is served topped with chopped walnuts or almonds.

Quick cinnamon, anise or clove tea

Make tea in the usual way and then add a pinch of ground cinnamon, ground anise or ground cloves. Anise tea is normally served sweet.

Honeyed coriander tea

For each person put half a teaspoon of ground coriander in a cup and add 2 teaspoons of honey. Pour over boiling water, stir, allow to settle, and drink.

Almond milk

4 oz (100 g) blanched almonds   16 fl oz (450 ml) water
4 oz (100 g) sugar   8 fl oz (225 ml) milk

Put the almonds, sugar and half the water in an electric blender and combine until smooth. Strain through a fine sieve and add the milk and remaining water. Chill and serve.

Yoghurt drink

This is a refreshing summer drink popular in many countries of the Middle East

1 pt (575 ml) yoghurt
½ pt (275) water
pinch of salt

Beat the ingredients together in a blender or bowl and serve very cold over an ice cube.

For a sweet drink, use sugar instead of salt.

Sherbet (sharbat)

Sherbets are sweet fruit syrups served very cold on their own for sipping or as a drink with iced water or soda water (fizzy sherbet). They can also be used to pour over ice cream or for making milk shakes. Fresh fruits such as cherries, strawberries, raspberries, blackberries, apricots and grapes are used.

Put the fruit (stoned if necessary) and an equal weight of sugar in a large bowl. Mash the fruit slightly and mix well. Cover and leave overnight, or for 6 to 8 hours at least. Strain the mixture through a muslin bag or fine sieve until all the syrupy liquid has been drained off. Bottle the syrup and store in the refrigerator. Serve 1 or 2 tablespoons in a glass of iced water.

If apples are used they must be peeled and grated first. Also add a squeeze of lemon juice to the mixture to prevent discolouration.

WEIGHTS AND MEASURES – ENGLISH AND AMERICAN EQUIVALENTS

English	American	Alternative
2 pt	2½ pt = 5 cups	
2 tablespoons	⅛ cup	1 fl oz (1½ tablespoons American)
8 tablespoons	½ cup	
1 pt	2½ cups	20 fl oz
½ pt	1¼ cups	10 fl oz
10 oz almonds, unblanched	2 cups	
8 oz ground almonds	2 cups	
9 oz apricots, dried	2 cups	
14 oz aubergines, diced	2 cups	
1 lb butter	2 cups	
8 oz bulgar wheat	2 cups	
10 oz sliced courgettes	2 cups	
14 oz chick peas, dried	2 cups	
8 oz chick peas, cooked	2 cups	
8 oz grated cheese	2 cups	
1 lb dates	2 cups	
9 oz wholewheat flour	2 cups	
8 oz white flour	2 cups	
14 oz lentils, dried	2 cups	
14 oz lentils, cooked	2 cups	
12 oz diced onion	2 cups	
4 oz finely chopped parsley	2 cups	
1 lb dry rice (brown or white)	2½ cups	

English	American	Alternative
1 part dry rice by volume		2 parts cooked rice by volume
8 oz sesame seeds	2 cups	
1 lb spinach, cooked	2½ cups	
1 lb spinach, uncooked	10 cups	
13 oz red beans, dried	2 cups	
13 oz red beans, cooked	2 cups	
1 lb granulated sugar	2 cups	
12 oz brown sugar	2 cups	
1 lb tomatoes		3 medium tomatoes
18 oz tinned tomatoes	2 cups	
18 oz tomato paste	2 cups	
1 oz fresh yeast	½ cup	
8 oz chopped walnuts	2 cups	
1 lb vegetable oil	2 cups	

METRIC/IMPERIAL CONVERSION TABLE

Ounces/fluid ounces (oz/fl oz)	Grammes or millilitres (g or ml) (to the nearest unit of 25)
1	25
2	50
3	75
4	100
5	150
6	175
7	200
8	225
9	250
10	275
11	300
12	350
13	375
14	400
15	425
16	450
17	475
18	500
19	550
20	575

OVEN TEMPERATURES

Temperature gauge	°F	°C	Gas mark
very low to low	200 to 300	93 to 148	¼, ½, 1, 2
medium low to medium	300 to 350	148 to 176	3
moderate	350 to 375	176 to 190	4
medium high to high	375 to 450	190 to 232	5, 6, 7
very high	450 to 500	232 to 315	8, 9

ARABIC/ENGLISH COOKING TERMS

This short glossary of Arabic words is given mainly for interest, but it could be of practical use if you are travelling in the Middle East or eating in a Middle Eastern restaurant. Colloquial rather than classical Arabic spelling is used.

Specific foods

almonds	*loz*	flour	*taheen*
apricots	*mishmesh*	food	*akl*
aubergines	*beitinjan*	garlic	*toom*
bananas	*moz*	grapes	*inab*
broad beans	*foul*	green beans	*fasouliah khadra*
butter	*zibda*	haricot beans	*fasouliah*
cabbage	*malfouf*	honey	*asal*
cake	*ka'ek*	jam	*tatli*
cauliflower	*arnabeet*	lemons	*lamoun*
cereals	*huboob*	lentils	*adas*
cheese	*jibneh*	macaroni	*ma'akaroni*
chick peas	*hummus*	marrows	*kousa*
cracked wheat	*bourghol or bulgur*	melons	*shumman*
(wheat		milk	*haleeb*
boiled,		mint	*na'na'*
dried, and		mushroom	*fou-oh*
crushed to		olive oil	*zeit-zeitoun*
one quarter		olives	*zeitoun*
of its size)		onions	*basali*
cucumbers	*khiar*	orange	*mazaher*
dates	*balah*	blossom	
desserts	*tihlai*	water	
dough	*ajeen*	oranges	*burtucal*
eggs	*beid*	pine kernels	*snobar*
figs	*teen*	(shelled pine	
		nuts)	

potatoes	*batatah*	tomatoes	*bandora*
rice	*ruz*	vine leaves	*warak-dawali*
rosewater	*maward*	walnuts	*joz*
semolina	*smeed*	yeast	*khameereh*
spinach	*silek*	yoghurt	*laban*

General foodstuffs and cooking methods

baked	*bilfouron*	sherbet	*sharbat*
boiled	*maslouk*	soup	*shoraba*
bread	*khubz*	stew	*yakhneh*
cooking	*tabeekh*	stuffed	*mahshi*
drinks	*mashroobat*	sweet pastries	*ka'ek hilou*
fried	*makli*	tea	*shay*
grilled	*mashwi*	Turkish	*halkoum*
meat	*lahmeh*	delight	
pickled	*makbous*	vegetables	*khoudra*
salad	*salatet*	water	*maay*
savoury pastries	*ka'ek maleh*		

Herbs and spices

basil	*reehan*	parsley	*bakdounes*
cardamom	*hab-hal*	pepper	*falafel*
chillis	*filfel*	pimento	*filfel akhdar*
cinnamon	*irfeh*	sage	*maryamiyyeh*
cloves	*krounfol*	salt	*milh*
coriander	*kouzbara*	sesame	*sumsum*
cumin seeds	*kammoun*	sugar	*sukkar*
nutmeg	*joz-teeb*	thyme	*za'atar*

BIBLIOGRAPHY

Turkish Cookery, Nezih Simon, Tredolphin Press, 1968

Kitchen in the Kasbah, Irene F. Day, André Deutsch, 1976

In a Persian Kitchen, Maideh Mazda, C. Tuttle, 1960

The Israeli Cookbook, Molly Lyons Bar-David, Crown, 1977

Moorish Recipes, Marquis of Bute, Oliver & Boyd, 1954

The Home Book of Turkish Cookery, Venice Lamb, Faber & Faber, 1969

The Flavour of Jerusalem, Joan Nathan and Judy S. Goldman, Little Brown & Co., 1974

Middle Eastern Cookery, Eva Zane, 101 Productions, 1974

The Armenian Cookbook, Rachel Hogrogian, Atheneum, 1978

Turkish Cooking, Irfan Orgh, André Deutsch, 1971

Lebanese Cuisine, Madelain Farah, Madelain Farah, 1972

The Art of Syrian Cookery, Helen Corey, Doubleday & Co. Inc., 1962

A Book of Middle Eastern Food, Claudia Roden, Thomas Nelson, 1968 (also a Penguin paperback)

Rayess' Art of Lebanese Cooking, George N. Rayess, Librairie du Liban, 1966

101 Arabian Delights (a Book of Arabic Cooking), M. J. Philipose, Clifton Books, 1969

Middle Eastern Cooking, Patricia Smouha, André Deutsch, 1955

The Best of Near Eastern Cookery, Ann Seranne and Eileen Gaden, Doubleday & Co. Inc., 1964

INDEX